A BOOK FOR PARENTS:

INTEGRATING EARLY CHILDHOOD DEVELOPMENT IN
BALANCE WITH TECHNOLOGY AT HOME

A. B. MAGEE, M.A.

A BOOK FOR PARENTS:

Integrating Early Childhood Development in Balance with Technology at Home

What comes first: Early Childhood Development or Technology? Discover the appropriate age to introduce your child to technology without risking their natural and necessary early development.

A.B. Magee, M.A.

ISBN: 979-8-218-27334-7 - paperback

ISBN: 979-8-88759-539-9 - ebook

Printed in the United States of America.
Cover Designer – Kelley Moreno
Editor – Noel B. Martin
To schedule a presentation, book signing event or for more
information go to https://www.abmagee.com; contact authorabmagee@gmail.com

This Book is Dedicated to
All the Children of the World
and
My Supportive Husband, Family & Friends

CONTENTS

A NOTE FROM THE AUTHOR

Greetings Parent

First, I want to thank you and express my deep appreciation for acquiring this book. I am very excited that you have an interest in understanding the importance of early childhood development in balance with use of electronic technology for your child. Your choice to seek information on how you can contribute to your child's healthy development will be of great value.

I am from California and working with families and their children has been my heart and soul for the last forty-nine years. In 1974, I was in my early twenties and volunteered for a Head Start program while working towards my bachelor's degree in Early Childhood Development. During this time, I also studied child development abroad in the United Kingdom, Denmark, Scotland and Sweden. As a teacher from my mid-twenties to early forties, I taught K-12, owned a private school, served as a board member for the Southern California Association for the Education of Young Children (SCAEYC), served as a trustee for a local school board and completed my higher education with a master's degree in Psychological Counseling and School of Psychology. After completing graduate school, I worked as a social worker and a consultant for 25 years, until my retirement.

Throughout my years as a teacher, I taught several grade levels including preschool programs that involved varying educational approaches such as: Whole-Person Learning, High Scope, Child-Centered Learning, and Montessori. During my 20 years of teaching children, I also came to realize their learning not only took place at school but also through reinforcement from home, with parents—their first teachers.

Because of this realization, I intended to write a book specifically for parents. At first, the content of this book was to explain the basic concepts of early childhood development from birth to 8-years-old, along with descriptive activities parents could use at home with their young children. Now, forty-nine years later I maintain the same vision. However, over the years, as technology became more widespread, I observed more and more technology taking over our educational systems and less focus on supporting an interactive, child-centered curriculum that stimulates our children's growth and development at an age-appropriate pace. True, technology is here to stay and will continue to advance, but it is likewise important to understand the necessity for young children to be able to master their basic developmental abilities and skills that foster creativity, imagination and critical thinking, along with a healthy self-esteem and confidence that prepares them for future academic learning and a technology-rich world. Thus, I was inspired to expand the content of this book, which I hope will give parents some insight into the benefits of balancing early childhood development experiences and the use of technology for their very young children.

And so, in the upcoming chapters, the primary focus is to discover the right balance between what young children need for their healthy development and our world of increasingly advanced technology. Specifically, my goal is to provide parents with information about how they can support their young children's physical, social, emotional, cognitive, and language growth, all of which are crucial to their development, as well as how technology can be integrated into their child's life in an appropriate and timely manner.

While my goal and vision is to inspire you to contribute to your child's early developmental growth at home, I hope the information on early childhood development and research on technology presented in the following chapters will provide valuable insights into how too much electronic technology too soon, can adversely affect a child. Likewise, I hope the art recipes and directions I share for creative arts and crafts will support your efforts to promote meaningful and purposeful learning at home. The list of simple and cost-effective materials will also make these activities affordable and fun to make. Again, my sincere thanks and gratitude!

INTRODUCTION

Your child's lifelong success begins during early childhood. By supporting their development during this period, you have the potential to impact their future. During their tender years, your child will begin to explore their environment, learn verbal and reasoning skills, and develop relationships with others. These familiar changes, and others, reflect your child's development in several essential areas. These essential areas include cognitive, language, physical, social and emotional development which are necessary to nurture the healthy growth of your child. Given how important the first eight years of a child's development are for lifelong success, it is especially important that parents and caregivers understand how to support their young children as they grow in our increasingly technology filled world. This book is designed to help you do just that, whether you are a parent, step-parent, grandparent, guardian, or extended family member caring for a young child.

Thompson and Rudolph (1996) pointed out that normal childhood development tasks include achieving independence, learning to relate to peers, developing self-confidence, forming basic values and mastering new ways of thinking. However, with schools increasing the use of technology in the early-grade classrooms, it is important to balance that with early childhood development experiences for young children to benefit from a curriculum that includes hands-on and active learning. American

Child Psychologist, David Elkind discusses the pros and cons of technology in education and cautions that technology "can be a curse as well as a benefit." He further details the importance of self-initiating and spontaneous play that contributes to a child's healthy cognitive, emotional and social development, that appears to be decreasing, while introducing technology in the classroom is increasing (Elkind, 2007).

It is my intention to provide you with the necessary and essential information in chapters 1 through 3 that will help you understand what is age-appropriate for your child and the necessity to balance early childhood development with electronic technology in your child's life. I have also provided you with a glossary of basic child development terms with simple definitions. This glossary will also help you understand the objectives of what your child can process and learn from the activities presented in chapters 4 through 6. A summary of the chapters are as follows:

Chapter 1 provides a summarized introduction to basic child development, describing the ages and stages of cognitive development according to Jean Piaget, a Swiss psychologist, well-known for his work on child development.

Chapter 2 discusses research findings and journals from professionals and educators who are from various parts of the globe, along with their recommendations regarding early childhood development and electronic technology use by young children. This chapter also emphasizes the importance of balancing these two concepts for your child's successful developmental growth and early learning.

Chapter 3 introduces and explains the different learning styles that children naturally develop to learn and process information throughout their lifetime, even as adults. This chapter also discusses how a parent can identify their child's learning style.

Chapter 4 provides ideas about setting up the home environment for age-appropriate activities and establishing routines that invite fun and participation in home learning for your children and the family. This chapter also provides a list of suggested tools, materials and recyclables that can be gradually collected for hands-on activities and includes how to organize and store them.

Chapter 5 contains a variety of basic art recipes that can be made with your child and used for a number of different activities as well as suggestions on how to store and preserve them for future use.

Chapter 6 presents a collection of activities along with what materials you will need to prepare for each of them. This chapter also provides an activity's developmental objective--the learning goal, for example, improving sensory-motor skills, in addition to instructions to present the activity to your child.

CHAPTER 1

AGES AND STAGES OF EARLY CHILDHOOD DEVELOPMENT

Many of us know that children develop in stages, but when these stages occur and what they include is not as widely known. This is unfortunate, given how powerful this information can be for anyone involved in supporting a young child's healthy development. I first discovered the value of this information when I began my study of early childhood development at the university. Once I started working with children, I was able to develop curriculum, consciously make observations of my young students in the classroom and assess their progress. It was because of my knowledge of childhood development, that I had the opportunity to discuss with parents any concerns they had, regarding their child's skills or abilities and worked together to develop an open-ended plan to address and re-evaluate those concerns. It is my belief that the foundational information on cognitive development to be discussed in this chapter, can help parents to understand the importance of their child's healthy developmental growth and consider this information, when making choices to introduce their young child to technology.

While there is an abundance of information about early childhood development, one foundational starting point is Jean Piaget's theoretical framework, regarding cognitive development. Since early on, in my career of working with young children, I had adopted Jean Piaget's framework and found it very valuable as a tool or guide. Though Piaget's theory can be very complex, his fundamental framework has been used as an introduction to cognitive development in colleges and universities worldwide. It is my hope that parents will find Piaget's framework beneficial and worthy as a guide or tool to observe their young child grow and flourish. The following is a brief introduction to Jean Piaget and his theoretical framework of cognitive development including, a brief review of his four stages of cognitive development.

Jean Piaget's Cognitive Development Framework

Jean Piaget Ph.D. was a renowned and influential Swiss developmental psychologist, whose work established a separate field within child development (Feldman, 2003). During the course of his career, from about 1920 to 1979, he engaged in research on the intellectual development of children—that is he investigated the processes by which intelligence and knowledge are acquired. Additionally, through his years of research that included observations and clinical interviews of children from birth through adolescence, Piaget identified "schemes" or thought patterns, which he considered the basic building blocks, or cognitive structures, of intelligent behavior – a way of organizing knowledge (Feldman, 2004; McLeod, 2018). Through his years of research on children's intelligence, in 1936 Piaget formulated his theoretical framework of cognitive development—four stages that are sets of mechanisms by which knowledge can be achieved between infancy and adolescence, with each stage laying a firm foundation for the next (Feldman, 2004; Gongala, 2022; Borst, 2022). Piaget's theory also establishes that all children across the globe and across cultures, pass through the sequence of stages and follow the same unchanging order, but not all at the same rate (McLeod, 2018). His theory emphasizes that the average age at which children go through each stage can vary considerably, from one social environment to another, or from one country or even a region within a country to another (Bybee & Sund, 1982; Piaget, 1972). Even in considering children with special needs, an article on special education by Suzanne Weekly (1979), pointed out that exceptional children develop Piagetian skills and concepts in basically the same sequences as non-exceptional children, however, the differences are the rate at which stages are achieved and new skills learned (Kaleta, 1975; Cowan, 1978).

Regardless of Piaget's influence, several critics have argued that his theory did not take into account social differences such as ethnicity, socioeconomic status, technologies, spiritual beliefs or family culture and traditions. Piaget acknowledged that he was not so much interested in the individual and their differences one to another, rather, he was interested in the common patterns of intellectual development that are shared by all. Thus, the intention of his theoretical framework was to show that each individual is fundamentally the same as every other individual when it comes to the kinds of cognitive structures that are developed. Piaget further declared, that even though social circumstances, due to change or advancement, could play a significant role in the formation and speed of cognitive structures in various ways, it basically did not affect the process (Feldman, 2003; Feldman, 2004).

Jean Piaget's Stages of Cognitive Development

Stage	Age	Goal
Sensorimotor	Birth to 24 months	Object Permanence
Preoperational	2 to 7-years-old	Symbolic Thought
Concrete Operational	7 to 11-years-old	Logical Thought
Formal Operational	12 to Adulthood	Abstract Concepts

(McLeod, 2022)

Sensorimotor Stage

According to Piaget, the first stage of cognitive development is the sensorimotor period. The primary purpose of this stage is for an infant to interact with the environment, through their senses and physical movement, which contributes to their development of intelligence—cognitive development. Furthermore, it is a period of rapid cognitive growth, that lays the foundation for the infant's further development (Bybee & Sund, 1982).

Piaget also describes an infant's progression of cognitive development in six sub-stages toward the goal of object permanence—the infant realizes that an object continues to exist, even if they cannot see it, as the following:

Stage 1. Reflexes (0-1 month): The infant does not differentiate objects from self and also has no concept of objects; there is no concept of what exists, only action. During this substage, an infant's innate reflexes of rooting, sucking, grasping and reaching are functions, ranging from sucking on nothing to sucking or grasping objects, such as a thumb or blanket. Likewise, the infant will innately, root--find a mother's breast to suck on a nipple for feeding.

Stage 2. Primary Circular Reactions (recurrent patterns) (1-4 months): The infant begins to actively involve their own body in some form of repeated activity but without purpose. At this substage, objects are now real, but only when visible to the infant. Further, the infant's sense of what exists is limited to the self, their senses, and in terms of time, they are only interested in the present moment.

Stage 3. Secondary Circular Reactions (4-8 months): The infant can now manipulate objects using their body, in order to make something happen. For example, they might make multiple attempts to pull a toy, or shake a toy to make sounds. These actions indicate that they are becoming more object-oriented. This is also the first hint of intelligent behavior, that implies a basic idea that an object does exist. The infant will also search for a partially hidden object but not for a completely hidden one. This behavior suggests some understanding the object continues to exist.

Stage 4. Coordination of Secondary Circular Reactions (8-12 months): The infant starts to show practical intelligence through the coordination of existing thought patterns to achieve a planned goal, indicating some understanding of what exists. For example, if an infant sees a toy under a dining room chair, crawls toward it, then reaches for and grabs it, then the infant has achieved a specific goal. Also, at this substage the infant has an idea of object permanence and is able to actively search for a fully hidden object. However, if the hidden object is moved to another hiding place, the infant is unable to find it. Additionally, by the end of this substage, the infant begins to walk, and so they become more mobile, better able to move, explore and experiment, in and with their environment.

Stage 5. Tertiary (3rd) Circular Reactions (12-18 months): The toddler develops actions that modify former schemes, creating new thought patterns and behaviors and adapting to new situations. Additionally, the toddler is now able to use motor skills and thought to carry out a planned goal with intent. An example of this substage includes the toddler who previously explored an object by taking it apart but now also tries to put it back together. Also, the toddler's knowledge of what exists is more refined and is now able to follow and search with intent, for objects that have been moved continuously from one place to another. Such reactions occur close to the end of the sensorimotor stage, around the beginning of the toddler's 2nd year (Bybee & Sund, 1982).

Stage 6. Onset of Representational Thought (18-24 months): The toddler shows intelligent actions and now fully achieves object permanence, meaning that they understand that objects, including other people, exist separate from the self and continue to exist even when they cannot be seen. The toddler's early symbolic thought emerges as they begin to refer to concrete objects, events or people, in the forms of gestures, sounds or a single word, as a means of their expression. At this substage, the toddler also shows early signs of representational thought and imitation by using objects symbolically, while at play. For instance, a small wooden block may become a telephone, an empty box may be used as a car or a train or a doll may become "mommy" (Bybee & Sund, 1982).

Preoperational Stage

Children from age 2 enter the preoperational stage of cognitive development until age 7 years-old and begin to build on skills they learned during the sensorimotor stage. During this period, between the ages of 2 and 4, the child breaks through their limitations of infancy, as they undergo tremendous growth and development. This is also a time of the greatest language growth when children begin to describe people, events and discoveries from their environment and to express their wants and feelings with words. By the age of 5, the child's social interactions move beyond their immediate family, they develop skills in formal language as well as self-care skills, including dressing, toileting, grooming and bathing (Bybee & Sund, 1982).

Additionally, the child in the preoperational stage is able to perform physical actions, using their memory, imagination and symbolic thought. For example, a 2-year-old child is able to move an object by thinking before moving it and then combine several actions to create a new behavior. Similarly, the child acquires basic symbolic reasoning abilities and learns to use words and pictures to represent objects in the real world, as well as to express their fears and anxieties.

Typically, a child in the early preoperational stage is also considered an egocentric thinker, as they assume that all people view the world as they do, since they view themselves as the center of existence. A child in this stage does not understand that someone else's opinions can be different from their own point of view. A child with egocentric thinking can have a possessive attitude about their belongings and you will often hear expressions of "No", "Me", "Mine" and "My" as part of their vocabulary. Additionally, at this stage, children's attachment to symbols helps to explain the difficulty they display when asked to share persons or objects they consider their own. For instance, sharing "mommy" with a newborn sibling or a favorite toy, could be difficult for a child in the pre-operational stage, because they think of the person or toy as a part of themselves and so it is like sharing a part of their being. However, most children overcome this egocentrism between 5 and 7 years of age, as their language development increases and they engage more in cooperative play with other children (Elkind, 2007; Bybee & Sund, 1982).

During this stage, play is an important part of a child's cognitive development. Through pretend or imaginative play, children assign roles, feelings and ideas to dolls, stuffed animals or other symbolic objects (wooden blocks, Lego's, etc.). Children often use these objects to express, explore and work out their own ideas and feelings, while at the same time they are learning through play. Furthermore, children will engage in pretend play such as role-playing store, doctor or dress up, include an imaginary friend at a tea party, use a box to represent a car, bus or train, pretend a stick is a sword or that a broom is a horse or imagine they are a superhero, while engaging in their own "pretend" dialogue. Piaget described this type of play, as "representational thought" through pretend dialogue, that contributes to a child's increasing development of language (Cherry, 2022; Elkind, 2007; Bybee & Sund, 1982).

Despite the importance of pretend play, children at the beginning of this stage are unable to play cooperative games because they will not yet follow the required rules. Rather, they will engage in play by themselves or side-by-side with other children their age, also known as *parallel play*. It is not until around 4 years of age, when they will become more interested in social interactions and start to enjoy structured games with rules (Bybee & Sund, 1982).

Piaget also points out that children up to the ages 3 or 4 years are often animistic in their view of the world--meaning that a child believes that almost everything is alive and that inanimate objects, such as toys, furniture, plants and animals have human characteristics, which is common in young children (Bybee & Sund, 1982; Mcleod, 2018).

During this stage, children ages 4 to 5-years-old are able to classify objects more than one way, by size, shape, color and texture. Even so, children at this stage will not be able to comprehend the concept of *conservation*-- a logical thinking ability that allows a person to determine that a certain quantity will remain the same despite adjustment of a container's shape or size. For example, a small ball of clay remains the same amount, even as it changes form when rolled out flat. Children in this stage also have difficulty with *reversible thinking*, because they prefer learning in ascending order before descending order, which means the idea of something beginning with the smallest and ending with the largest, rather than in reverse, that something begins with the largest and ends with the smallest. For example, a child may be able to count forward but not backwards (1 up to 5 but not 5 down to 1). This is also a reason why a child at this stage is not yet capable of completing mental operations of reasoning or logic, such as mathematical processes. Instead, the sensorimotor and preoperational stages prepare children for future mental operations, including math, logic and critical thinking. So, by the time a child is 6 to 7 years of age, they are on the verge of transitioning from the pre-operational to the concrete operational stage of cognitive development (Thompson & Rudolph, 1996; Bybee & Sund, 1982).

Concrete Operational Stage

The concrete operational stage serves as an important transition between the preoperational and formal operational stages for children from ages 7 to 11-years-old, that is characterized by increasingly more sophisticated thinking such as logic and emerging mental operations. Children are now mature enough to use logical thought through inductive reasoning (a logical process that involves using experiences or observations to identify patterns and make a general conclusion) but, they are only able to apply this logic to physical objects or situations with direct experience. This is why even though children in this stage might still struggle with abstract ideas (an idea that does not have a physical or concrete form), they are able to logically conclude that if every dog they have ever seen, barks, then all dogs must bark (Cherry, 2021).

According to Piaget, children in the concrete operational stage are able to apply emerging mental operations that include reversibility, classification, seriation and conservation, which continues to develop into early adulthood. One important development in this stage is that children begin to understand the concept of *reversibility*—that is, they recognize that actions can be reversed. Unlike most who are in the preoperational stage, children in the concrete operational stage are now able to reverse in ascending or descending order, although some might still have difficulty with descending order (5 down to 1). They are also able to identify the properties of categories, to relate categories or classes to one another and use this information to solve problems through *classification*. Piaget points out that one of the important processes that children develop during this stage is that of *seriation*, which refers to the ability to mentally sort or arrange objects or situations according to any characteristic, such as size, color, shape, type, volume, height or weight. Similarly, children in this stage develop their ability to comprehend the concept of *conservation*. That is, they understand that when a substance (e.g., a specific amount of liquid or clay) changes in shape or appearance, it remains the same and has no effect on its mass, number, volume, or length (Bybee & Sund, 1982).

Piaget further emphasizes that during the concrete operational stage, children's ability to perform simple mathematical operations starts to unfold. But first, they must be able to demonstrate and explain their understanding of the concept of *number*. At this stage, for children to reach the understanding of *number*, will depend on their coordination of seriation and classification which leads to the understanding of number. He also points out that, although most children in the preoperational stage were able to count, they did so without understanding the meaning of *number*. Whereas children in the concrete operational stage, can show an understanding of *number* when they can explain the number of objects involved, order and classify them. As children transition through this stage, they gradually begin to develop the ability to perform certain mathematical operations. By the end of this stage, they will typically, be able to perform simple math operations such as addition, subtraction, multiplication and division (Bybee & Sund, 1982).

The concrete operational stage is also marked by a decrease in egocentrism. Children at this stage are able to move beyond thinking that they are the center of reality and that all people view the world as they do. Instead, they are able to consider and appreciate the viewpoint of others (Thompson & Rudolph, 1996; Cherry, 2021).

Lastly, children in this stage are able to recognize the difference between reality and fantasy. Their interest in playing pretend decreases between the ages of 6 and 8-years-old and they become less likely to believe in fantasy characters, like Santa Claus or the Easter Bunny. Later on, between the ages of 8 and 12 years-old, children become increasingly focused on realism and seek to understand the real world through their toys, games and other activities. To be clear, fantasy continues to exist, for children at this stage, but the main point is that they understand the difference between the two concepts (Vinney, 2022).

Formal Operational Stage

The formal operational stage is Piaget's fourth and final stage of cognitive development that begins at 12-years-old and lasts into adulthood. Both concrete and formal operations have to do with the development of logical thought, which is useful for mental operations like mathematics. Between the ages of 12 to 15 years-old (early to middle adolescence) the adolescent begins to think like an adult, becomes increasingly abstract in their thinking, processes reversibility more effectively and is able to imagine the outcome of certain actions (Thompson & Rudolph, 1996; McLeod, 2010).

At this stage, logical thinking abilities such as deductive reasoning, and systematic planning emerge. As previously discussed, children in the concrete operational stage are capable of inductive reasoning but are still not able to engage in abstract thinking, because they are only able to apply logic to physical objects/situations with direct experience. Whereas, the adolescent's increased development of logical thinking, no longer depends *solely* on inductive reasoning, rather, it is combined with deductive reasoning. The main difference between inductive and deductive reasoning is that, while inductive reasoning begins with observations to identify patterns and make a general theory, deductive reasoning begins with a theory, supports it with observation and eventually formulates a valid conclusion. For example, if theory A says that all humans live on land and theory B says that Mark is a human, the conclusion that one would get from deductive reasoning says that Mark lives on land--because Mark is a human. Also emerging, is the adolescent's ability to systematically solve a problem in a logical and methodical way. At this stage of cognitive development, they are often able to plan an organized approach to solving a problem. In sum, adolescents in this stage gradually develop more complete coordination of mental processes (Lynch, 2021; Bybee & Sund, 1982).

Lastly, it is important to emphasize that, according to Piaget, not all adolescents approach the formal operational stage. As previously discussed in this chapter not all children move through the stages at the same rate. Likewise, the ability for logical thinking can vary considerably for adolescents in this stage, since their transition from the concrete to the completion of the formal stage can continue well into adulthood. Piaget points out that adolescents can demonstrate patterns of reasoning that have both concrete and formal operational elements--meaning they will demonstrate concrete thought consistently and formal thought inconsistently (Bybee & Sund, 1982).

Summary

As I mentioned at the beginning of this chapter, Piaget's theory of cognitive development, can be complex and hope the above summarized information will be a useful tool or guide for parents or for anyone raising children from birth to 8 years of age. With this in mind, I have purposely provided you with more details for the sensorimotor, preoperational and concrete stages, as these are the periods of tremendous development that are foundational for a young child's life-long learning. This is not to say that the formal operational stage is insignificant, however, since this book's focus is on early childhood development, I have given this later stage less emphasis. Regardless, as you look closely at the transitions children make from one stage to another until early adulthood, you may notice a progression of gradual development that leads to increasingly sophisticated processes of thinking, which appears in Piaget's last two operational stages.

While Piaget's theory involves stages with specific age ranges, it is important to understand that young children do not magically transition from one stage to another at the same rate. Rather, there are many factors that can influence whether a child transitions on target, in terms of Piaget's age ranges, spends more time, developmentally, in one stage or advances to another stage more quickly. These factors can include biology, environment, culture, social norms, religious practices, socioeconomic status and family practices that can vary from family to family as well as one country or even a region within a country to another. Additionally, your child's physical health can be another factor that might influence how they progress through these stages of cognitive development that can include premature birth or other birth-related health concerns, genetic disorders or other disabilities.

So, you might wonder, what does electronic technology have to do with the theory of cognitive development? As explained in this chapter, cognitive development for young children involves activity using all of their senses, including movement of their bodies that allows them to learn through their environment, in order to reach their natural growth. Whereas, electronic technology only provides learning and receiving immediate feedback by the *click* of a *mouse* and involves sitting in front of a laptop, television or other type of screen monitor without any physical use of their whole body. Now I want to be very clear, I am not promoting an *either-or* option here, rather my intended message is that it is important to understand the importance of early childhood development experiences along with *how, when and why* to introduce electronic technology to your young child and the need for balancing the two.

A main point I want to emphasize is that young children need to have real-life social and active learning experiences within their environment, in order to develop their cognitive skills and stimulate their curiosity, creativity, discovery, imagination, as well as language and other significant domains of development. As you read on through the next chapters, you will find this main point commonly emphasized for consideration when making choices to balance early childhood development with the use of technological devices in your home. In the best interest of your child, it can be enlightening when making these choices, to consider the point of view from various professional experts on this topic.

For decades now theorists, psychologist, neurologists and other educational professionals, world-wide, have questioned and expressed concerns of how too much technology too soon could have harmful effects on children's learning. The next chapter provides you with both the pros and cons on the use of electronic technology for young children by several professionals from various countries in the form of studies, articles and journals along with their outcomes, conclusions or opinions on this subject matter.

CHAPTER 2

AGE-APPROPRIATE INTERACTIVE
LEARNING AND TECHNOLOGY

Since the mid-20th century, many of us have witnessed the rapidly growing use of computers and other electronic devices in our homes, schools, and workplaces. Whether for entertainment or educational purposes, we are now surrounded by technology such as digital software program applications (apps), streaming media, children's TV programming, the internet, e-books, smartphones, tablets, CDs and other media and electronic devices. Understandably, parents and educators have become concerned about the impact of computers and electronic devices on the development and education of young children. These concerns guide the questions that are the focus of this chapter: Can computers and other screen media meet the necessary developmental requirements for young children, while preparing them for the future and its continued technological advances? Is there a need for a better balance between interactive learning that encourages hands-on experiences, exploration and creativity in all areas of a child's early development and the use of technology?

I have reviewed several studies, articles and journals, from the late 1990s to 2022 from various countries, which provided the pros and cons of the previously mentioned inquiries yet, not all of studies presented, concluded with total consensus and instead, expressed a need for further research and investigation. Even so, it is my intention to summarize the key findings and information provided by these experts in a manner that I hope you will find useful and informative. I also hope this will help you think about your own experiences with your children's early development and their use of technology in the home. The five essential areas (domains) of early development for young children that will be covered in the following information includes *cognitive, language, social, emotional and physical development.* I also invite you to use the glossary provided for you near the end of this book, to look up the meaning of any technical terms that are used in the following content.

Early Childhood Development and Technology

A study from Scotland, by Plowman L & McPake J (2013), focuses on clarifying myths that technology in the home has adverse effects on a young child's cognitive and social development. This study, focuses on 3 and 4-year-olds and their parents' views, examines which technologies children engage with and how family cultural practices influence their use of technology at home. The researchers use multiple methods such as observations, child-led home tours and shared discussions with parents and children to gather information and outcomes. Although there are seven myths that Plowman L & McPake J (2013) focus on for their study, only five relevant myths will be discussed in this section, as they are directly related to the topic of this book and include the following:

Myth #1: Childhood and technology should not mix.
Parents point of view about this myth differ. However, all parents agree it is important for very young children to balance the use of technology such as computers, cell phones and other technology-based activities with traditional means of play such as games, books and outdoor activities. Reports from the majority of parents show there is no evidence that technology has any damaging effect on their young child's behavior or learning.

Myth #2: Technology hinders social interaction.
The premise of this myth suggests use of technology in the home hinders

children's involvement and communication with their families. Parents report that when, as a family, they all participate in viewing digital media and engage in discussion of such experiences, they believe their child is motivated to develop their own narratives and creative responses. The end results show that with parental support and guidance, thoughtful use of digital media could enhance their child's social interaction rather than obstruct it.

Myth #3: Technology dominates children's lives.
This myth points out that most households have some form of screening technology in the home that is used every day and children do not spend enough time playing. The majority of parents report that they are aware of the dangers for their children to spend too much time with technology. Nevertheless, parents report they are relaxed about the time their children spend on electronic technologies in the home and they do not believe this is a problem for their family.

Myth #4: Play equals learning.
The premise of this myth is how much children learn through play with technological devices. This study suggests that children can learn through use of technology in the home, if there are opportunities to combine play and learning by developing an awareness of family cultural practices. For example, providing children with an old computer or other non-operating device as a prop to engage in pretend play, could extend an opportunity for learning and imaginary play for young children.

Myth #5: Children need to get tech savvy for their future lives.
This myth premises that children need to learn to use technologies at an early age. Some parents believe this to be true, to prepare their child for the future. However, other parents from this study argue there is no benefit because any technologies would be outdated by the time their child reaches adulthood. Moreover, concerns from other parents are that their young child will become too involved with technology instead of more valuable use of their free time. So, while it is important to prepare

children for the future, there is no certainty what technical products will dominate the workplace in the far future.

Ultimately, Plowman and McPake conclude that young children's experiences of playing and learning with various technologies could inspire learning, especially with the support and encouragement from adults in the home. The end result shows that most parents prefer that their children engage in and enjoy a balanced range of hands-on activities and experiences along with scheduled time spent on technology-based activities.

Healthy cognitive and social development--two of the five essential areas of early development for young children, are critical. Kimberly Kneas, Ph. D. and Dr. Bruce Perry, Ph. D., an internationally recognized authority on brain development and children, discuss in an interview, whether children ages 3 to 6 are well suited to using technology. According to Dr. Perry, modern technologies such as television, videos, and most computer programs which are visually-oriented, are passive and are not beneficial to the essential areas of emotional, cognitive, physical and social development needed for young children. However, Perry points out that modern technologies can be beneficial when they are interactive, allowing children to interact in a way that helps them to develop their curiosity and thinking skills. Also, he notes that some children with special needs, like those with fine or large motor problems, may have difficulty writing neatly. Thus, a computer word processor program can be beneficial to them when they need to complete a writing assignment for school, while also helping them with spelling and strengthening their self-esteem and confidence at the same time.

Furthermore, Perry explains that even though interactive computer programs can be positive for young children, they must be introduced at the *right time*, meaning that their healthy development is, first, dependent on enriching and interactive real-life experiences, as well as nurturing interactions with real human beings. He further adds, that children need an integrated and well-balanced set of experiences to grow socially and intellectually into capable adults, which is why balance and timing is key to healthy development. Similarly, he points out that the key to technologies that are beneficial, are those that expand a child's meaning of their world, as it must enhance their social development as opposed to any potential social isolation (United States, 1999).

The importance for a child to have interactive real-life experiences is expanded in an article by Jason Burns, a research associate from Michigan State University, who discusses technology and the development of social-emotional skills for young children (2016). His discussion is in response to a 2015 report issued by the World Economic Forum (WEF) on social-emotional learning that concludes, young people must be equipped with technology-related skills to fully participate in 21st century society. The WEF report argues for more potential technology in education (education-technology) that could serve as tools by educators or parents, to foster social and emotional learning and complement and extend the learning experience.

Burns offers a critical response to this WEF report and its conclusions. He argues that technology is unlikely to be a central part of a young child's development of social and emotional skills. He claims that while it may serve as a complement to learning such skills, education-technology lacks the human-to-human element and sensory engagement present in real-life interaction. He further argues that use of machines (e.g., computers) are not as effective at promoting skills such as creativity, curiosity, leadership, problem-solving, and critical thinking, since the situations and tasks that nurture those skills are difficult to computerize. Moreover, education-technology is less effective at promoting these skills since developing them requires the human contact necessary, to learn to work with each other and to succeed in any challenges one could socially encounter. Burns concludes by endorsing his support of a people-driven approach vs a technology-first approach for a young child's development of social and emotional skills.

The benefits of a people-driven approach are not limited to social and emotional development. In a recent review, Mary L. Courage, Ph. D. and Georgene L. Troseth, Ph. D., who are from Memorial University, Canada and Vanderbilt University, USA, agree that infants and toddlers have an increasing access to screen media such as television, computers, smart phones and tablets and are responsive to its features such as, movement, pace, bright color, music and sound effects. Courage and Troseth report that, since infants and toddlers learn by imitating their parents and older children, swiping a tablet or cell phone does not mean they understand or learn from the device's content, because their language and comprehension skills are limited (2016).

Moreover, for infants and toddlers, content from screen media is symbolic that differs from reality which, due to their tender age, they are not yet able to know the difference between these two concepts. In contrast, 3-year-old children, whose essential areas are further developed (i.e., language, social and emotional development), are more flexible learners and are able to transfer meanings from screen media to the real world. Courage and Troseth also report concerns that time spent on screen media could be less beneficial to infant and toddler development, if it replaces interactive social and language learning activities and play. Similarly, there is a concern that an infant and toddler's use of screen technology could be harmful to their development of attention, self-control and possibly affect learning, which is why pediatricians discourage screen technology for children under the age of 2-years-old. Furthermore, the evidence also suggests that the amount of time a very young child spends on screen technology is associated with poor executive functioning and other cognitive processes crucial to a strong foundation for effective learning (2016).

Many infant-directed videos target word learning, however, researchers found little evidence of word learning for infants younger than 2-years-old from a baby video, even with a parent co-viewing with their infant. With regards to how much screen time is too much for this age group, Courage and Troseth suggest that it depends on the characteristics of the child, the design and effectiveness of the program's content, and the quality of their learning environment (2016).

Courage and Troseth conclude there is little evidence of learning that takes place, when children under the age of 2 or 3-years-old view screen media, especially if they are watching alone. They recommend that children from this age group learn best from interactions with others, listening to story books, exploring their environment and playing with toys. They suggest the best thing parents can do to support effective development for their infant or toddler is to talk, read, and play with them. However, if they do allow their young children to view screen media, it would be best to do so together, in order to increase any learning potential (2016).

While it is often easy for parents to recognize the importance of reading and talking with their children, knowing that it benefits their cognitive development and early learning, the value of play-based learning can be less obvious, yet just as significant. An article from the Encyclopedia on Early Childhood Development, by Angela Pyle, Ph. D., from OISE, University of Toronto, Canada, titled *Play-based Learning: The Joy of Learning Through Play* (February 2018) premise that play-based learning is a teaching strategy that is important for early childhood development. Learning through play influences the development of a child's social, emotional and cognitive abilities and fosters their academics skills. Pyle explains that for very young children, play is the pathway to early learning, as it is the most natural and best way for them learn through mental activity, exploration, and useful interaction with materials.

Pyle describes two types of play: *Free play* is child-directed, voluntary and unstructured. It is also stimulating and beneficial for the development of social competence and self-regulation. *Guided play* is led by a child and an adult and tailored for a specific learning goal. An example of free play is a child engaging in pretend or make-believe play that encourages use of their imagination--for instance, using a small building block as a telephone. Similarly, an example of guided play is when an adult provides specific learning materials in the home or classroom, that are chosen by the child for the purpose of learning a particular skill, such as a Memory or Bingo game and is guided by an adult.

Pyle further explains that since increasing numbers of children are active users of in-home technical devices, parents are encouraged to be attentive of the amount of time their children spend on digit media and game programming. At best, there should be a balance between the amount of digital play and more traditional playful activities, such as imaginary play, outdoor or other hands-on activities. This requires parents to prepare an environment that contributes to play-based learning opportunities for young children, such as providing materials for arts and crafts, blocks, books, puzzles, costumes and other toys that draw out a child's natural curiosity, creativity and willingness to explore new possibilities through play.

Pyle concludes that this concept of play-based learning is relatively new, and more research is needed. The level of adult guidance that promotes developmental and academic learning that meets the needs of young children from different backgrounds needs further consideration. In addition to the benefits for parents to make time and space for their young children to play without screen media, the same is true for physical activity.

An article from Hello Motherhood, by Anne Reynolds, titled *The Physical Impact of Technology on Children* (United States, December 2018) premises that while a child's mind is engaged on a computer, the active use of their body is limited. Reynolds describes the importance of balancing a young child's use of technology with physical activity to promote physical and social development, in order to prevent potential health issues such as obesity and to develop friendships with peers. Also, since young children learn through imitating their parents, Reynolds suggests they demonstrate to their child that it is okay to withdraw from technology and to make time for physical activity. For example, parents can turn off the TV during dinner time, limit the time spent on technology and participate in some form of physical activity as a family.

Besides the concern of too much screen time impacting a child's physical health, it is also important to be aware of other impacts it can have on a child's behavior. An article from The Conversation written by Jackson A. Smith and Dillon Thomas Browne, from the University of Waterloo, Ontario, Canada, *Is Your Child Addicted to Screens? Here's What You Can Do About It* (July 2019) premise that when someone is addicted, the source of their addiction becomes their priority. Likewise, other important life activities such as sleeping, eating and bathing are neglected and a decrease of interests for playing sports or spending time with family and friends, become factors of concern. When the source of the addiction is cut off, this can trigger an intense emotional reaction. Generally, behavioral addictions do not apply to children under the age of 12-years-old. Therefore, if a young child were to have a meltdown in response to turning off a digital device, this would not be an indication of addiction.

According to Smith and Browne, many clinical scientists claim human beings can be addicted to screens, while other prominent researchers argue that digital addiction is a myth. However, Smith and Browne note that they do take parents and children's concerns seriously when presented with worries about problematic media use. The authors also explain that the issue of screen addiction is complex due to the large number of screens available that include smartphones, tablets, laptops, televisions (TVs), a wide variety of social media, TV shows and video games, as well as the fact that they can be used either actively or passively. Moreover, since addiction is a chronic condition of dependency, research shows it is important to determine if there is a genetic or social component, like stress, that may contribute to addiction. Even so, the increased risk for addiction does not mean that one is destined to become addicted.

Smith and Browne offer parents recommendations for screen-time limits published by the Canadian Pediatric Society in 2017, to promote healthy screen use for young children under the age of five that includes: No screen time for children under the age of 2-years-old; less than one hour per day of screen time for children two to five-years-old; avoid screen time at least one hour before bedtime; and maintain daily screen-free times for reading books and family time.

Likewise, Smith and Browne offer parents recommendations for screen-time limits, published by the Canadian Pediatric Society in 2019, to promote healthy screen use for school-age children and adolescents that includes: Managing screen use with individualized time; content limits and learning; co-view and talk with your children and teens to help them to choose age-appropriate content; discourage use of multiple devices at once; discuss appropriate online behaviors; and encourage meaningful screen use to prioritize daily screen-free routines over screen use. Parents can also model healthy screen-free use by turning off their own media screens when they are not in use. Most importantly, parents must monitor for signs of problematic use such as, oppositional behavior in response to screen-time limits and use that interferes with sleep, school, face-to-face interactions, offline play and physical activities. Smith and Browne encourage mindfulness of how we all integrate the various technologies into our lives and of the consequences they can have on ourselves, our relationships and our children.

Teachers from other parts of the globe also express their concerns of how digital learning in their classrooms may impact their students. A study from Stockholm, Sweden conducted in 2015 is presented by Anthemis Raptopoulou Ph. D., an education lecturer at the Stockholm University in Sweden, in her article, *Preschool Teachers' Perspectives and Use of Digital Game-based Learning* (2020). The goal of this study is to explore the use of digital games in preschools in Sweden and focuses on preschool teachers regarding their perspectives (opinions) and the use of such games in the schools where they work. The objectives of the research are to explore: what are the teachers' perspectives on digital game-based learning (DGBL) and whether their opinions have any effect on the use of games; how digital games are selected and used by the teachers; and whether there are any barriers to their use. The data was gathered through informal interviews, using open-ended questions, with preschool teachers from the region of Stockholm.

An analysis is made from interviews with 7 Stockholm teachers who work either in public or independent preschools. They are represented in two categories: those who are positive towards the use of Digital Game-based Learning (DGBL) in the classroom and those who are more skeptical about the use of digital games in preschools.

The group of teachers who had a positive perception of DGBL, believe it is important for the children to interact with digital tools in a digital society--a society that has adopted information technologies, which the teachers use to complement their teaching methods. This group of teachers also include other teaching methods such as playing with physical tools and learning how to use their bodies, as a means to balance any effects from digital games. They do this through controlled use of digital devices under their guidance and establish time limits and usage rules. Lastly, these teachers also report that the use of digital media is a fun tool for children to learn, as well as an additional resource that is of interest them.

The group of preschool teachers who were more skeptical towards using DGBL consider themselves to be against digital game use for early childhood education, as they believe DGBL promotes antisocial attitudes and isolation. Instead, they prefer the traditional use of books, physical tools, and oral communication in their classroom. This group of teachers also view digital games as an obstacle to the development of children's social and emotional skills and they believe there is more focus in receiving information quickly versus engaging in social interaction. Regardless of the opinions from the two groups of teachers, it is important to note that all the teachers were in strong agreement about one thing: children should not play with DGBL without adult supervision and guidance.

Raptopoulou concludes that since this study was done in 2015, in mid-2018, a new curriculum for Swedish education was promoted to strengthen digital education from the first grade of primary school. She suggests further research is needed to compare the updated digitalization trends that emerge in Sweden's formal education settings, including teachers' perspectives and use of DGBL

Excessive use of technology can impact other areas of a child's development. An article from The Tot, by Anastasia Moloney, an Early Childhood Development Specialist (United States), presents her view in *Technology Impact on Child Growth & Development* (2022). She points out that, when used correctly, technology can have a positive effect on a child's behavior and development. However, when it is not properly controlled, there could be negative effects from too much screen time in some areas on a child's development such as critical thinking and attention span.

Moloney points out that studies have shown a decrease in daily reading, due to increased use of technology and other researchers have also argued that digital devices do not challenge a child's critical thinking skills or expand their thought processes. She recommends that in order to encourage critical thinking, it is important to set aside time each day for reading books without electronics. By engaging children in conversation about what they read or heard in a story, parents can promote critical thinking as well as help their child to build conversation skills.

Additionally, Moloney notes that attention span development is affected by environmental factors and with so many forms of technology available, children are often more distracted when devices are close at hand. Also, excessive visual stimuli from devices and a lack of story reading could impact a child's development of creativity which is why it is important to provide children with books that inspire them and develop their imagination.

Moloney also points out that beyond reading, imaginary play is crucial to a child's healthy development. When a child engages in this type of play, not only does it provide them with opportunities to develop their thinking and problem-solving skills, but it also helps them develop their language skills as they actively experiment with the social and emotional roles of life through role-playing.

Although social media can be used to maintain existing relationships, Moloney emphasizes that it is important to give children plenty of opportunities to practice verbal communication and social skills without technology. In conclusion, Moloney recommends for parents to clearly understand that technology should be used as a learning tool and should not be a substitute for real-life interactions. This point is especially important, as there can be long-term negative effects for children who are allowed excessive use of technology, with a notable growing reluctance to interact with other peers in real-life social environments.

Summary

You might recall that I began this chapter with two guiding questions: Can computers and other screen media, meet the necessary developmental requirements for young children, while preparing them for the future and its continued technological advances? Is there a need for a better balance between interactive learning that encourages hands-on experiences, exploration and creativity in all areas of a child's early development and the use of technology? Based on the above information, it is clear that educational and other experts the world over are increasingly concerned with similar questions—so much so that they were driven to use their expertise to conduct studies and publish articles or journals that address their concerns about how electronic technology can affect early childhood development. Even though there is no global consensus *for or against* the use of technology by young children, these experts generally offer a common recommendation: what is best for a young child's early development is a balance of real-life social interactions and age-appropriate hands-on activities along with the reasonable inclusion of technology.

Therefore, the best way for parents to promote the healthy development of their very young child is to provide them with a variety of activities that encourages play. Maria Montessori, one of the last century's most brilliant educators, coined a phrase "play is the work of children" and Jean Piaget, famously declared "play is work." The messages from these two prominent figures from past centuries, helps parents and educators alike, understand and develop the mind-set that play is essential for children, as it contributes to, and is required for, their natural development and early learning.

Bearing that in mind, parents can guide and support their child's early learning development by providing their 2 to 5-year-old child with activities such as listening to stories from books, promoting play with age-appropriate toys, arts and crafts, blocks, puzzles, and other materials that facilitate imaginary play and learning through creativity, curiosity, exploration and discovery. Additionally, parents can provide outdoor activities for their children to develop physically while also promoting other important skills like, eye-hand coordination and bilateral coordination, as well as other real-life, hands-on activities that help young children naturally achieve the essential areas of cognitive, language, social, emotional, and physical development. These types of activities, at any given time, can promote the development of other important skills, such as critical thinking, communication, problem-solving, attention span, executive functioning, and reasoning skills, all of which are important in preparing children for academic learning once they reach school-age.

Academics aside, parents who actively engage in reading books, outdoor or hands-on activities with their children, will find that it strengthens family communication and bonded relationships. Of course, how this unfolds will vary across families, depending on factors such as culture and home situations, but one, two or more hours set aside for family time at least once each week will be of great value, benefiting not only the young child and their development but also the entire family. Given the information provided in this chapter, it should be clear just how important it is for parents who are a child's first teachers, to make sure their young children, first, have real life experiences and interactions with human beings in order to support their healthy and natural development. Although it is recommended that parents avoid using technology with children under the age of 2-years-old, if their choice is to allow a very young child to use electronic technology, it is essential to set time-limits as well as to guide and supervise their children's usage.

The bottom line is for parents to understand that basic early childhood development is essential for all young children. Moreover, balancing this with technology usage is of utmost importance, since it provides the necessary foundation for children to develop into competent and healthy adolescents and ultimately, successful adults. How parents apply the concepts and principles presented in this chapter can vary, depending on their family's belief systems, worldviews, economic status and cultural practices, and will likely vary from country to country.

Whatever method parents use to apply these concepts and principles will also vary, depending on how their child learns. With that in mind, in the next chapter I will provide information that can be used as a guide, to identify the learning style your children develop which helps them to effectively process information to learn.

CHAPTER 3

IDENTIFYING YOUR CHILD'S LEARNING STYLE

The familiar fact that every child is unique reminds us that, what works well for one child may not be the same for another. This might seem obvious when a child learns to walk, talk, or socialize and it is also true as they take in and process information. To put it another way, every child has an individual learning style of their own. Most likely, there are many parents, who have recognized their own style of learning. By identifying their child's learning style, parents can nurture and support their strengths and interests. With that in mind, this chapter presents a well-known framework for understanding learning styles and also offers tools for identifying learning styles in children. Hopefully, you will find this information helpful as you support your child's learning both at home and school.

While learning styles and their importance have been recognized since at least the 1890's, the specific styles and accompanying framework discussed in this chapter were developed by educational theorist Neil Fleming in 1987. He designed these concepts to help make sense of how different individuals receive and retain information when they learn. Since its creation, Fleming's framework continues to be widely used, discussed and investigated by experts in education and psychology (Cherry, 2019).

The term *learning style* refers to the different ways in which children process, remember and learn information. As discussed in chapter 1, young children in the sensorimotor stage, learn through all of their senses, primarily through hands-on experiences of touching, playing, moving, seeing, tasting, smelling and hearing. Even after young children start to develop their language skills and begin to have richer social interactions with family members and others, they will typically, still learn through all of their senses.

However, by around age 4-years-old, they will begin show early signs of how they learn best, favoring one or two senses when processing and receiving information. Since there are various ways to learn effectively, it is essential for parents to discover what works best for their child. Parents can begin to identify their child's learning style just by observing how they interact with toys, learning tools such as, books, art supplies, play equipment and audio equipment, as well as, how they interact socially (Fairchild, 2016; Perlson, 2022).

In the rest of this chapter, I offer a brief discussion on learning styles, some of their traits, and suggestions to help you identify your child's preference for learning. This awareness can place you in the best position to advocate on behalf of your child, in school and more effectively support your child's interests and learning at home.

Types of Learning Styles

A child's sensory preferences will determine their natural learning style, whether it is visual, auditory, kinesthetic-tactile or any combination of the three. According to many experts in the field of education and psychology, children are born to be kinesthetic, since movement, experiencing and taking in information through all of their senses is necessary for their early development. However, around the age of 4-years-old, a child's preference for visual and auditory learning styles begins to emerge. The benefits of understanding the different types of learning styles is that it will provide parents the necessary information that will be helpful to support their child's learning needs (Perlson, 2022; Lipoff, 2011).

Visual	Learn through sense of sight, observing, pictures or images
Auditory	Learn through sense of hearing/listening, sound and verbal information
Kinesthetic-Tactile	Learn through whole body physical movement, sense of touch, hands-on, writing, drawing, building with hands

Visual Learners

Children who are visual learners tend to be watchful of what is happening around them and they are good at absorbing information through their sense of sight. Hence, a child is considered a visual learner if they appear to understand ideas or information more easily through watching what others are doing or by looking at pictures, symbols or images, than by learning through their other senses (Hilton, 2020; Putri, 2022). Since they tend to focus on details visually, they can notice minute similarities and differences between objects and people and can easily engage in imagery, which can influence their strong ability for memory. Given their preferences, visual learners tend to understand better when *shown* how to complete a task (Fairchild, 2016; Singh, 2022).

Furthermore, since visual learners think primarily in pictures and images, they greatly enjoy visual stimulation. Even more, they tend to have a strong sense of color, which can contribute to their artistic or mechanical talents, as well as highly creative imaginations. In addition to this, visual learners tend to be highly organized, and neatness may be a priority for them as they need to be able to easily see what they need (Hilton, 2020; Singh, 2022).

To the contrary, visual learners can face challenges when verbal instruction or directives are the main source of receiving information, since this can interfere with their concentration. As a result, their minds may begin to wander, and they will often not remember information if they cannot see it. Furthermore, visual learners process verbal input slowly because they must convert it, to visual imagery (Weebhoys, 2008). Thus, what is most important to recognize, is that visual learners need to see things in order to understand and remember them.

Auditory Learners

Children who are auditory prefer to absorb information through hearing and through sound. They have strong listening skills, would rather have information explained verbally to them, and tend to have strong critical thinking, comprehension, verbal and communication skills, Auditory learners enjoy and prefer to learn and understand information, by listening to or telling stories or engaging in storytelling activities such as role-playing (Afrebo, 2022; Bay Atlanta University, 2022).

Additionally, the auditory learner enjoys conversations and learns best in groups with other children (Putri, 2022). They may also frequently talk to themselves, whether they are solving problems out loud or reading aloud, since this helps them to process and remember information better (Afrebo, 2022; Putri, 2022; Hilton, 2020; Cherry, 2019). Similarly, auditory learners typically enjoy listening to music and many show a knack for playing musical instruments, as they have a strong sense and ear for music, due to their ability to hear the different aspects of a tune (Afrebo, 2022; Christina, 2021).

In contrast to the visual learner, auditory learners are challenged when having to process large amounts of detailed written information, instructions, or visual illustrations and might find that they need verbal explanations for clarification. They may also have difficulty absorbing information in activities that involve long periods of reading and writing. Furthermore, due to the auditory learner's sensitivity to sound, noisy environments can make it difficult for them to concentrate (Afrebo, 2022; Bay Atlanta University, 2022). In sum, what is most important to understand is that auditory learners need to hear information in order to learn.

Kinesthetic-Tactile Learners
Kinesthetic

Children who are kinesthetic learners appear to be in constant motion, they like physical movement, and learn best through experience, moving, and doing. Therefore, they are physically active and hands-on learners who learn through their bodies, like using their sense of touch to process information, and need to actively explore their physical world. Most kinesthetic learners excel in motor memory (Roell, 2020) which can contribute to cognitive processes, as a result of engaging in physical activities such as running, swimming, dancing and other sports (Leisman, Moustafa & Shafir, 2016). They also have great eye-hand coordination, high levels of energy and enjoy experimenting (Roell, 2020).

On the other hand, because kinesthetic children learn through movement, sitting still and listening to others for long periods of time will be difficult for them. They can also become bored and lose focus, when required to read or write for extended periods of time (Fleming, 2020; Wilson, 2022). In short, they learn best when engaging in physical activities and manipulating objects.

Tactile

Similar to kinesthetic learners, children who are tactile, also learn through touch. Specifically, they prefer activities or projects that allow them to use their hands, as they learn best through fine motor movements rather than whole body movement (AbilityPath, 2020). So, a tactile child may enjoy scribbling or drawing with markers, pens, chalk and so forth, or painting with brushes, sponges or other tools. Other common characteristics of tactile learners include enjoying field trips as well as projects and tasks that involve manipulating materials such as cooking, crafting, and making art. In short, these children learn best when using their hands to create.

Combination of Learning Styles

As previously discussed, learning styles include visual, auditory and kinesthetic-tactile. It is important to recognize that, as a young child approaches middle school age, they may begin to show more complex preferences for learning (Mann, 2007). That is, they may prefer a combination of learning styles. So, as much as it is valuable to understand your child's preferred style for learning, it is also important to provide a young child with a variety of learning experiences to help them become well-balanced learners. By honoring a child's learning preferences, while also encouraging experimentation and exploration in learning, parents can address the challenges that might arise for their child and simultaneously contribute to their child's future as a successful and capable adult.

Observation to Identify Learning Styles

As discussed in previous chapters, many children develop at their own rate and some experts have recommended to start observing and evaluating to identify a child's learning style from 4 to 7-years-old (Mann, 2007; Fairchild, 2016; Perlson, 2022). Based on early observations, parents can determine which learning experiences are engaging, interesting and most beneficial for their child. Furthermore, as parents observe their child over time, there might be a noticeable change in their learning preferences until they reach middle school-age. The reason being, a child's skills and abilities further develop and their learning styles become more defined, which is an important consideration (Mann, 2007). Once you have identified your child's learning style, you will be better prepared to provide the support and help they need to reach their full potential (Wilson, 2022). To identify your child's learning style, you might begin by considering the following questions (not limited to) for making observations:

Auditory Learners

- Do they prefer quiet activities?
- Do they like to read books aloud or often ask to read them a story?
- Do they seem to be fascinated with numbers and patterns?
- Do they have great rhythm?
- Do they enjoy listening to music, humming, singing songs or playing musical instruments?
- Are there certain types of activities where their attention span is clearly shorter or longer?
- Do they enjoy activities that require verbal interaction?
- Do they enjoy listening activities?
- Do they prefer to listen to information rather than read it in written text?
- Are they good at connecting with people through conversation and humor?
- Do they prefer verbal direction rather than being shown how to do something?
- Are they good listeners?
- Do they have a good memory for names, details, and parts of conversations?

(Afrebo, 2022; Lipoff, 2011; Roell, 2019; Wilson, 2022; Zing, 2021; Hilton, 2020; AbilityPath, 2020; Christina, 2021; Bay Atlantic University, 2022)

Visual Learners

- Do they like to draw or paint pictures?
- Do they prefer to be shown how to do something rather than being told verbally?

- Do they enjoy being social with relatives or friends, or do they feel more comfortable being
- alone and engaged in a quiet activity?
- Do they like to use their imagination and create their own activities? Do they like to create a
- story about their activity?
- Do they quickly learn and recognize shapes, colors and letters?
- Do they favor routine/dislike change, or do they favor spontaneity, change, and new
- experiences?
- Do they like to learn with visual images or symbols?

(Singh, 2022; Fairchild, 2016; Zing, 2021; Lipoff, 2011; Roell, 2019; Wilson, 2022; Hilton, 2020; AbilityPath, 2020; Putri, 2022)

Kinesthetic-Tactile Learners

- Do they like activities in which they move or are otherwise physically active?
- Do they have difficulty sitting still for long periods of time?
- Do they enjoy dancing, running, biking or other sports activities?
- Do they favor outdoor or indoor activities?
- Do they enjoy building structures with small objects like wooden blocks, Legos, or empty boxes?
- Do they enjoy stringing or twisting things together?
- What types of activities cause them frustration?
- Do they like to take things apart and then try to put it back together?
- Do they like touching and feeling objects?
- What types of toys do they prefer?

- Do they like painting, cooking, mechanics, sports or woodworking?

(Lipoff, 2011; Roell, 2020; Wilson, 2022; Hilton, 2020; Ability-Path, 2020; Putri, 2022; Cherry, 2019)

Additionally, you might consider asking others what kinds of activities they have observed your child enjoying including, relatives or extended family, other caregivers, parents of your child's friends who see your child frequently and teachers. You can also consider sharing some or all of the above questions with those who know your child well (AbilityPath, 2020).

Summary

By introducing learning styles in this chapter, I hope to have provided you with a valuable guide for understanding how your child takes in and processes information. Equally important, I hope this information helps you recognize what motivates your child to learn and to have a strong sense of what types of engaging activities fit their interests and learning preferences.

In previous chapters, I emphasized how important it is to provide real life, interactive experiences for young children. Not only will these experiences support healthy development, but they will also give your child the opportunity to discover their interests and find out what makes learning fun. At the same time, these experiences will help your child develop their learning style and, in return, help you to identify their learning style.

Likewise, identifying your child's learning style can also be beneficial when it is the *right time* to introduce technology to your child, as previously discussed in Chapter 2. Most importantly, you will have the opportunity to be mindful of choosing electronic programming that stimulates, supports and honors your child's style of learning as well as save you from overly investing time, effort and resources. For example, if your child is an auditory learner, then you might do well to avoid educational media or technologies that primarily rely on visuals or large amounts of detailed, written information—instead, you might find that audiobooks, along with a book to follow the narrated story, serve your child much better. In contrast, for a visual learner, technologies and media that mostly rely on visual stimulation might be more engaging and beneficial.

Choosing media and technologies for the kinesthetic learner can be a bit tricky, as it can be difficult for them to sit for long periods of time, that screen-based media often requires. By specifically choosing technologies and media that require your child to move and use their bodies, you can honor their learning preferences and keep them engaged. For example, media or computer programs that offer demonstrations and then invite your child to practice the physical techniques for skateboarding, basketball or other sports might be especially effective.

Regardless of your child's learning style, the key point here is balance. Your child will be better supported as they learn and grow, when you integrate a balance of real-life interactive learning experiences, along with technologies that complement and engage their learning style.

To help you support the development of your child's learning style through hands-on activities from home, the next chapter will provide you with ideas and recommendations for setting aside purposeful family time and routine, including where and how to set up an early writing/literacy corner and the home environment for interactive learning activities, the difference between open-ended vs end-product activities and a list of suggested tools and materials.

CHAPTER 4

FAMILY TIME, ROUTINE, HOME SET-UP
FOR ART AND EARLY LITERACY
ACTIVITIES

Family Time and Routine

M ost parents and full-time caregivers strive to make family time a priority. Nevertheless, sometimes it can be challenging, especially if they work full-time 5-6 days a week and 8 or more hours per day. This means that weekends are typically reserved for household duties such as grocery shopping, cleaning the home, doing laundry, yard work, or catching up on what could not be accomplished during the week. Afterwards, parents and caregivers do what they can to spend some quality time with their family, whether it is having a meal at a restaurant, going to the movie theater, attending social functions--all in an effort to stay connected. In contrast, there are some parents and caregivers who work hard during the week and "play hard" on weekends that are filled with fun-packed adventures and experiences with their families.

Whatever your family's situation might be, the purpose of this chapter is presented with two thoughts in mind: 1.) The importance of establishing a family time routine that balances family involvement with activities that contribute to a young child's early development; and 2.) Excluding any involvement with media or electronic technology.

Many educators have observed in their classrooms, that young children thrive and feel secure with routine, as a child has no concept of time and tend to live in the moment. Likewise, most children feel safe and secure at home, because their parents may have set up a routine that has been accepted by all family members. With that in mind, parents can include family time to their routine by setting aside a particular day and time of the week, that engages the whole family in activities that are beneficial for a young child's developmental growth--and not only that, but doing so, also gives the child an occasion to look forward to. Whether family time involves engaging in an art activity, a trip to the library for story time or checking out books, a community event, a family picnic for dinner and play, a family hike, gardening, or other outdoor physical activities involving the family, these interactive experiences contribute to a young child's developmental growth and strengthens family relationships.

There is no doubt that life can be hectic, especially for working parents, so flexibility is essential, as situations can arise that will disrupt the family time routine. Regardless of the timing, the importance is for family time routine to involve the whole family. For example, if the choice for family time is an art activity, include everyone in the set up and clean up processes. This fosters collaboration, teamwork, inclusion, cooperation in the decision-making process, strengthens family unity and communication and supports learning for young children who are in preschool or Kindergarten (Spreeuwenberg, 2022)

The next section will focus on where and how to set up art activities in the home that promotes freedom for creativity, a young child's independence and imagination, and supports the five essential areas (domains) of early development as discussed in chapter 2.

Choosing an Area in the Home to Set Up Art Activities

As mentioned previously, choosing a specific time is as important as selecting a specific day, when it comes to establishing a family time routine. Therefore, if the family's choice is to engage in an art activity at home, it is best to set aside at least 1.5 to 2 hours that includes set up, the actual art process and clean up. Keep in mind, that the art process can vary, depending on the child's age, attention span and what is involved for a particular art activity.

There are several places in the home to consider for an art work area such as the kitchen, living room or dining room tables or another area of the home such as a garage or outdoor area. If possible, choose an area that is not covered with carpet or other absorbent material. If this type of area is not available, simply cover the area under a table with a drop cloth, old bed sheet or some other type of covering to protect against spills and stains. Accidents do happen, especially with young children! Also, for further protection, consider table coverings such as a used washable tablecloth (one that is okay to stain), plastic-coated place mats that establish workspace boundaries (optional), an old shower curtain, bed sheet, or other coverings that lays flat on the table or outdated newspapers with masking tape to hold the pages in place, are also a good option. They are easiest for cleanup—just roll them up and toss them into the garbage.

Wherever art activity setup takes place, it is helpful for the top of a table to be at the child's waistline, so the child can sit on a chair or stand and be able to easily reach for the materials in the middle of the table. This will support a child's independence to easily choose art materials without the distraction of having to constantly ask for help from others

Art Activities - Open-Ended vs End Product

The idea of providing art experiences that promotes a child's development of creativity and imagination lies in the open-ended process vs the end product of an art activity. This means that a child's thought process of what they envision in their mind, to create from their imagination, is more important than any specific end product, meaning a specific outcome of what the art activity "should" look like. For example, a printed copy of a blank picture of a face is given to a child and they are instructed to glue the cut outs of eyes, ears, nose and mouth onto the picture to create a face—the end product is a face with all its parts, in the right place. Whereas, open-ended art activities have no pre-determined limitations and no "right" or "wrong" outcome, which allows the process for imagination and creativity to freely flow.

Developmental art activities, such as those described in chapters 5 and 6, are considered open-ended and typically, have a developmental objective or goal for a young child, such as language development, eye-hand coordination, sensorimotor, or fine motor skills—only to mention a few. It is also important for parents to understand that children under the age of 6 years-old, learn more from the process of an open-ended art activity but fare better at end-product art activities, when they are older and their cognitive, language, and fine motor skills are further developed.

Most important, open-ended art activities allow for the development of a child's freedom to experiment, be creative, and develop their imagination. Likewise, open-ended art activities support a child's emotional development because the stress, anxiety or worry of having to complete their activity in a specific way, is not expected. As a result, their self-esteem and self-confidence flourish because, no matter how they end their art activity, it is fantastic and wonderful. On the flip side, young children who are forced into end-product type art activities, will typically experience frustration and will, eventually, demonstrate their loss of interest, as these activities limits a child's desire to explore and experiment with the tools and materials.

Another suggestion to consider, is to allow young children to engage in art activities without worry of messiness or soiling their clothing. Thus, providing aprons to protect their clothing is recommended. Consider the options of child size aprons made from cloth or homemade aprons from small sized plastic trash liners with cutouts for their head and arms. One more thought to consider, is to have the child wear clothes that are alright to get stained with paint, glue, etc., or have the child wear short sleeved tops or roll-up long-sleeved clothing, during art activities. Bear in mind that it will be difficult to keep young children attention during an art activity if they have to worry about staying clean. Nevertheless, there are young children who naturally do not like to get dirty. For these children, it is recommended to accept who they are and, simply and gently, let the child know there is no need to worry about spills or messiness. The idea is to set up a relaxed and worry-free environment without such concerns, in order to create a space for spontaneity, free flowing creativity and having fun.

Steps to Get Started

In getting started to set up an art activity, it can be difficult to know how to begin, especially, if this is a new experience. The chart below provides a condensed checklist to prepare for an art activity in the home and offers an outline that is easy to follow and can be added to.

Plan an art activity ahead of time	Choose from activities provided in chapters 5 and 6 or make up your own
Gather needed materials	Paint, glue, brushes, etc., flat trays such as meat trays, pie tins, egg carton lids, etc., anything that keeps various materials separated, depending on what is needed for an activity
Shut off phones, television and all devices	
Select music, children's music or music the child like (optional)	Low to medium volume to prevent having to talk over loud music during an activity
Table and Flooring coverings	
Child size aprons (optional)	
Tub of soapy water	Paper towels or clean old rags for handwashing that is reachable by the child.

Collecting and Storing Recycled Items for Creative Arts

Accumulating recycled materials for creative arts can be an on-going activity and fun for the whole family. This can include having a large paper bag next to a kitchen garbage container used specifically for materials that, once cleaned and dried, can be used for creative arts. Once family members have started collecting these items, do not be surprised if they find ways to include materials beyond the ones listed below. Whatever materials are collected, it is advisable to store them in separate, labeled plastic containers or used shoe boxes for purposes of organization and easy access. For example, labels can include: collage materials, yarn/string, jar/bottle caps, egg carton sections, small boxes (from bar soap, toothpaste, over-the-counter vitamin/RX boxes), fabrics, ribbons, small Styrofoam packaging and so forth.

Below is a starter list for parents, caregivers, and family members to start collecting:

Recommended List of Tools for Activities
List of Tools for Painting or Gluing

- feathers
- used sponges
- combs
- tooth brushes
- paint rollers(diff. sizes)
- rag strips(diff. widths)
- Q-tips
- scrub brushes
- straws
- eye droppers
- bottles w/ roller tops
- paint brushes (diff. sizes)
- potato mashers
- old shoe laces
- clothespins
- rubber spatulas
- spray bottles
- Bingo dabbers (lrg.)
- cotton balls
- bubble wrap
- old mascara brushes
- wine bottle corks
- nail polish brushes
- small wheeled cars

- small glue brushes
- small cans for glue/paint
- pie tins
- meat trays
- small yogurt containers
- plastic butter tubs/lids
- basting brushes
- handi-wipes
- spools
- cookie cutters
- string/yarn
- crumpled paper
- marbles
- large beads
- pipe cleaners
- golf balls
- baskets
- ice trays

List of Materials to Paint

All kinds of objects with varying surfaces:

- colored paper scraps
- newsprint
- gift wrap
- tag board
- butcher paper
- poster board
- construction paper
- finger paint paper
- cardboard
- foil
- toilet/paper towel tubes
- rocks

- drift wood
- sand paper
- Styrofoam meat trays
- burlap
- coffee filters
- boxes (various sizes)
- envelopes
- paper plates
- paper towels
- bubble wrap
- paper doilies
- suede/leather
- cellophane
- fabric (varying)
- wood (diff. shapes/sizes)
- textured wallpaper
- waxed paper
- cloth
- paper bags
- bark
- old place mats
- tissue paper
- vinyl
- egg cartons
- old screens

List of Ingredients to Add Textures to Paint or Glue

- sand
- coffee grounds
- Karo Syrup
- dish soap
- water (for consistency)
- rice
- sugar

- corn meal
- salt
- oatmeal
- soap flakes
- baking powder
- cooking oil
- shaving cream
- glue to paints
- liquid starch
- glitter

List of Medium for Creative Arts

- finger paint
- watercolors
- Popsicle sticks
- shaving cream
- colored pencils
- crayons (thick/thin)
- highlighters
- glitter pens
- colored glue
- gel pens
- clay
- tape (diff. colors)
- stencils (various)
- liquid starch
- flavoring extracts (scents)
- cookie cutters
- beads (various)
- hole punchers
- scissors (left/right)
- small rolling pins
- boxes (diff. sizes)
- popcorn

- paper plates
- food coloring
- tongue depressors
- empty spice container
- plastic strawberry baskets
- packaging
- used salad spinner
- old record player
- colored pasta
- small rulers
- plastic spoons/knives
- beans (various)
- rubbing alcohol
- used hot plate
- small cheese grater
- used iron
- measuring cup/spoons
- play dough
- scribble cookies
- marker pens (thick/thin)
- ink pads w/ stampers
- flour
- egg carton sections
- corn starch
- tempera paint (powder/liq.)
- chalk (pastels)

List of Materials for Collages and 3-D Art

- cut up straws
- yarn
- fabric scraps
- magazines
- greeting cards
- tissue/crepe paper scraps

- ribbon
- twine
- glitter
- colored egg shells
- used stamps
- confetti
- small wood scraps
- packaging materials
- bows
- streamers
- fringe
- fake fur scraps
- velvet
- wrapping paper
- popsicle sticks
- shiny paper scraps
- wallpaper books
- pompom balls
- googlie eyes
- paper doilies
- colored pasta/rice
- cotton balls
- Easter grass
- used catalogs
- buttons
- sequins
- feathers
- felt/lace/rickrack
- foil
- seeds
- shredded paper
- dried flower petals/leaves
- colored wire
- spools
- beads

- sea shells
- bottle caps
- pipe cleaners
- colored/glitter/glue
- cardboard
- colored tooth picks
- paper plates
- milk cartons
- egg carton sections
- cut paper toilet towel rolls
- colored sand/salt (powdered tempera paint)
- recycled containers (use as trays)

Early Writing/Literacy Corner

The previous subsection discussed children's art activities for family time, preparation and set up on a table, in an area of the home. Aside from that, the following discussion will focus on setting up a more permanent designated area in the home, for a child's early reading and writing activities, a place where they can do so independently and at their leisure.

Parents can support their young child's development of independence and skills for language development, eye-hand coordination, fine motor skills and early literacy, by designating a small space in the home to use, for these kinds of activities. Doing so, gives a child the opportunity, during their free time, to draw, write or read a book or engage in a quiet activity, of their choosing, with little or no supervision, depending on the young child's age. At best, this is most fitting for a child who is 2 years of age or older.

Once a parent sets up a writing/literacy corner, introducing the materials in this space will be necessary. For instance, if a child has never used crayons, other writing tools or paper, demonstrating and guiding them in how to use these items, will be helpful. Teaching a child how to use the materials will inspire them to explore, experiment and create, during their free time.

Likewise, it is recommended to use plastic containers or unused shoe boxes, to store various writing or drawing tools and label them with pictures, symbols or written words. This will help the child to recognize what materials belong inside a particular container. Once a child understands how to use these materials and where they belong, they will eventually, be able to select materials and put them away on their own.

To prevent a child from becoming overwhelmed with too many choices, it is recommended to make available materials and containers, a little at a time, and change them out every few weeks. Doing so, prevents a child's boredom or disinterest from lack of variety. By rotating materials, parents can encourage a child's interest and enthusiasm, for creativity with a wide variety of materials.

Area, Materials and Furniture for Early Writing/Literacy Corner

An early writing/literacy corner can be anywhere in a home's living space or in the child's bedroom. Recommended furniture includes a child-sized table and chairs, along with shelves to store the containers with writing materials, books, outdated magazines for cutting out pictures, puzzles, and perhaps a few table toys, such as Legos or stacking toys. By adding a large soft pillow or small bean bag in the area, parents can add a relaxing and comfortable feature the child can use to read a book.

Child sized table, chairs, and shelving can easily be found or made. Tables and chairs can be made by taking regular-sized tables or chairs that are no longer useful and cut the legs down to a child's comfortable height. In lieu of making child-sized furniture, garage sales and thrift stores can be a fun and inexpensive option—likewise with hand-me-downs from friends or relatives. Whether the furniture is made or acquired, it is worth noting that children are attracted to color, so painting a table or chairs with drizzled or brushed various colors of tempera paints can be a fun activity that involves the child to help create furniture they will want to use. To keep the paint in place, parents can later coat the table or chairs with a light varnish.

For shelving, consider building one with small to medium-length planks of wood and cinder blocks, or small crates. These can be used on the ends of the wood planks to create 3-to-4-tiered shelving, and the inside of crates, if used, can make great bookshelves. Other, inexpensive shelving can be found at garage sales, thrift stores, or made from an unneeded shelf that can be cut down to size.

Provided below is a list of suggested materials, for the writing/literacy corner, to store in labeled plastic containers or unused shoe boxes. Many of these items may already exist in the home, can be handmade, or can be inexpensively purchased at garage or yard sales, or at thrift or discount stores, such as a dollar or a 98-cent store.

Pencils, large and small crayons, chalk, colored pencils, glitter pens felt pen markers	Small tape dispensers with various colors of tape	Stamp pads (various colors) with various stampers
Sewing cards with various colored yarn for sewing (refer to Chapter 6 for making sewing cards)	Homemade stencils of shapes, patterns, letters for tracing	Various colored pipe cleaners for twisting together or other use
Writing pads	Small envelopes, used postage stamps	Child safety scissors - for right or left hand
Various stickers	Index cards – plain/colored	Various colored Bingo dabbers
Glue sticks	Small hole punchers	Various sizes, color, shapes of paper

Summary

The previous discussion on family time and routine is meant to expand or improve family relationships without the presence of technical devices for a few hours or more each week, in addition to providing a learning experience for all children in the home. It is important to encourage all family members in the process whenever possible and above all—have fun! I strongly recommend to set up an early literacy corner because having one somewhere in the home is especially beneficial for all young children, for all the reasons previously described in this chapter. The lists of materials for art activities shown above will help you get started and at some point, you will probably find many more to add to the list.

The last 2 chapters, 5 and 6, contain basic art recipes that can be used for a variety of open-ended activities and can also be applied to holiday or cultural events, along with a curriculum of hands-on activities. These chapters also describe what materials you will need for preparation and how to present them to a child

CHAPTER 5

EASY ART RECIPES FOR LEARNING
ACTIVITIES

<u>SLIME</u>

Materials:
- Bowl
- One part Liquid starch
- Two parts white glue
- Eye dropper
- Food coloring

Directions:
In a bowl, drip the starch *slowly into the glue* until the mixture becomes a workable ball. *If it is stringy--add a drop of glue. If too hard, add more starch.* Add color with food coloring using an eye dropper, *one drip at a time.* Experiment, combining primary colors to make a new color. Store in refrigerator in a covered container. Chill for 2-3 hours. Hands will stain when mixing in the food coloring, but after a couple hand washings the color in the hands will come off.

SILLY PUTTY

Materials:
- 2 small cups
- Glue 1 Tbs
- Epsom salts 1/2 tsp
- Water 1/2 tsp
- Measuring spoons
- Plastic spoon
- Waxed paper
- Plastic bag (optional)

Directions:
1. Put Epsom salt and water into one of the cups, stir with spoon to dissolve salt as much as possible.
2. In the other cup put glue. Add the Epsom salt and water mixture, from the 1st cup to the glue and stir.
3. The material will start to form. Pull out the putty and put it on the waxed paper. You can experiment with it and notice how it feels in your hands—smooth, sticky, etc.
4. Store the putty in a plastic zip lock bag in the refrigerator to keep it fresh for a few days. Wash hands and keep putty off carpets and furniture as it can stain.

GOOP

Materials:
- Large bowl
- 1 cup of cornstarch
- 1 cup of baking soda
- 1/2 cup of water (optional-add 1-2 drops of food coloring)

Directions:
Add cornstarch, baking soda and water into a bowl. Mix with your hands and feel the ingredients harden, soften and drip while you form and play with it. Wash hands with a soap and water.

DRIZZLE GOOP

Materials:
- Bowl
- Large spoon
- Flour 1 Cup
- Sugar 1/4 Cup
- Salt 1/4 Cup
- Water 3/4 Cup
- Food coloring (Optional)
- Eye dropper
- 2-3 recycled squeeze bottles

Directions:
Mix ingredients all together with a large spoon in a bowl. With an eye dropper, add 2-3 drops of food coloring to water (optional). Pour into squeeze bottles. Drizzle on paper.

PAPER MACHE' RECIPE

Materials:
- Large bowl
- Large spoon or spatula
- Liquid starch
- Water
- Newspaper strips

Optional:
- Small to medium sized balloons
- Thin, light weight wire formed into shape, animal or other symbol
- Beans, rice or other grain
- ¼ measuring cup
- Packaging tape
- Clothespins

Directions:

Mix equal parts of liquid starch and water in a bowl with spoon or spatula. Stir until starch is dissolved. Soak newspaper strips in liquid mixture, place wet strips to completely cover balloons or wired form. If you are using balloons, hang upside down with a clothespin on the tied end of the balloon and let dry completely. Once completely dry, pierce balloon inside covering with a pin and pull out from tied end of balloon. A small hole can be filled with a quarter cup of rice, beans or other grain and cover hole with a strong packaging to make a shaker.

<u>BAKER'S CLAY</u>

Materials:
- 1 large mixing bowl
- Measuring cups (glass)
- Salt 1 cup
- All-Purpose flour 4 cups
- Water 1½ cups
- Cookie cutters
- Various food flavorings
- small/medium size plastic/wooden spoon or spatula

Directions:

Pour flour into a large mixing bowl. Add salt. Add water. Mix ingredients with a spoon or spatula. Knead dough and form into various shapes or use cookie cutters to make shapes. Place shapes on a baker's cookie sheet lined with foil and bake at 350 degrees for about 1/2 hour or until baked thoroughly. Remove from oven and allow to cool. Paint when cool.

Mixing Techniques:

Allow the child to help as much as possible. Allow for spills. Encourage child to smell, feel and taste ingredients as you are making the baker's clay (before painting).

KOOL AID PLAY DOUGH

Materials:
- *Bowl*
- Flour (sifted) 2 – 3 cups
- Salt 1/2 cup
- Cooking oil 3Tbs.
- Kool-Aid (unsweetened) 1 pkg
- HOT water 1 cup

Directions:

Mix together flour, salt, oil, and Kool-Aid with spoon or hands. Add the cup of almost boiling water. Mix well. After cooling, knead the mixture until it forms a soft dough. Add flour or water as needed for desired texture. Store in a sealed container in the refrigerator.

<u>BIRD SEED FEEDER WITH PLAY DOUGH</u>
(Can also be made with peanut butter)

Materials:
- Birdseed 1- 2 cups
- Empty toilet paper tube
- Hole punch – small
- Strands of thin yarn or string
- Glue
- Glue brush
- Flour 2 cups
- Salt 1 cup
- Water
- Roller
- Small cookie sheet or large meat tray

Directions:
Mix flour, salt with sufficient water with spoon or hands to make play dough texture. Punch a hole on two top sides of the toilet paper tube, one directly across from the other. Brush glue lightly over the tube. Roll out a ball of play dough and cover the entire tube (do NOT cover punched holes). Roll and press the covered tube into a tray of bird seed, covering the entire tube. Gently shake off excess bird seed. Stand tube upright and allow to set for 1-2 days, to harden. Take 1 strand of yarn/string and lace through one of the holes and tie a knot and lace the other end of the yarn/string through the other hole and tie a knot. Hang bird feeder on a tree and watch birds feed.

SAND PLAY DOUGH

Materials:
- Bowl
- 1 part white glue
- 2 parts flour
- 2 parts sand
- 2 parts water

Directions:

Mix ingredients together in a bowl with spoon or hands to create a dough. You may need to add more water or flour depending on the consistency. Store in a sealed container in the refrigerator.

MOON CRATERS

Materials:
- Bowl
- Liquid Starch ½ cup
- Rock Salt 2 cups
- Glue with food coloring/Tempera paint ½ cup

Directions:
Mix liquid starch, rock salt and colored glue in a bowl with spoon or hands. This makes a gooey, rocky mixture. Make several batches of different colors. Mixture can be piled over other colors of mixture on cardboard or other surface to make 3 dimensional structures.

PEANUT BUTTER PLAY DOUGH

Materials:
- Bowl
- Spatula or serving spoon
- Creamy peanut butter 2 cups
- Rolled oats 2 cups
- Dried milk powder 2 cups
- Honey 2/3 cups

Directions:

Mix all ingredients with a spatula or serving spoon until thoroughly combined. Knead small portions with hands and roll into small balls. Makes a great healthy snack with milk or juice. Storage: When not using, MUST be stored in an airtight container.

COFFEE PLAY DOUGH

Materials:
- Bowl
- Large spoon
- Used coffee grounds 2 cups
- Cornmeal 1 ½ cups
- Salt ½ cup
- Water ½ cup and add as needed
- Flour add as needed

Directions:
Mix all ingredients in a bowl until pliable. Knead with hands and add water and flour as needed to achieve a working consistency. Store in a sealed container in the refrigerator.

SALT PLAY DOUGH

Materials:
- Bowl
- Large spoon
- Salt 1 cup
- Water 1 cup
- Flour 1/2 cup

Directions:

Except for the flour, mix remaining ingredients into a bowl, pour into a saucepan and cook over medium heat. Remove from heat when mixtures look thick and rubbery. As the mixture cools, slowly roll in flour until it cools into dough. Store in a sealed container in the refrigerator.

SOAPY PLAY DOUGH

Materials:
- Bowl 2
- Large spoon
- Flour 2 cups
- Salt 1/2 cup
- Liquid tempera paint 2Tbs.
- Liquid Dawn soap 1Tbs.
- Water 1/2 cup

Directions:
Mix all the dry ingredients in one bowl. Then mix the liquid ingredients in another. Combine and stir the two mixtures together and knead until pliable. Store in a sealed container in the refrigerator.

CLOUD DOUGH

Materials:
- Salad oil 1 cup
- Flour 6 cups
- Water 1 cup
- Food coloring or tempera

Directions:

Mix food coloring or tempera paint into water. Use just enough water to bind mixture. Knead until soft and pliable.

CHUNKY SCRIBBLE CRAYONS

Materials:
- Old broken crayon pieces without paper
- Muffin pan 6 section
- Cupcake liners for pan

Directions:

Put broken paperless crayons inside muffin tins (lined with cupcake papers). Place in warm oven at 200°. Let melt. Peel off paper liners when cool. Suggestion: Melt 2 colors together and see what happens.

SPARKLY SALT PAINT

Materials:
- Salt 2 cups
- Liquid starch ½ cup
- Water 1 cup
- Tempera paint or food color

Directions:

In a bowl thoroughly mix liquid starch, salt, and water. Slowly add tempera paint or food coloring. Use as paint. Pictures will sparkle when the salt paint dries.

COLORED GLUE

Materials:
- Recycled food can
- Glue
- Tempera paint or
- Food coloring
- Squeeze bottles

Directions:
Thoroughly mix food coloring or tempera paint and glue in a recycled food can. Pour into glue bottles.

<u>BUBBLE SOLUTION</u>

Materials:
- 3 cups water
- 2 cups Dawn liquid detergent
- 1/2 cup Karo syrup
- Container with lid

Directions:

Mix ingredients and use for making bubbles.

<u>HOMEMADE FINGER PAINT RECIPE</u>

Materials:
- 2 tablespoons sugar
- 1/3 cup cornstarch
- 2 cups cold water
- 1/4 cup clear Dawn dish soap
- Food coloring or food coloring paste
- Small containers to store finger paint (recycled baby food jars or small plastic containers).

Directions:
Mix together sugar and cornstarch in a small pan, then slowly add cold water. Cook over low heat, stirring until the mixture becomes a smooth, almost clear gel about 5 minutes. When it's cool, stir in clear Dawn dish soap. Scoop equal amounts of the mixture into containers and stir in food coloring or, for more vibrant colors, use food-coloring paste.

DYEING PASTA

Materials:
- Food coloring
- Various shapes of macaroni pasta, ½ to 1 cup per color (uncooked)
- Rubbing alcohol ½ to 1 cup per container
- Paper Towels
- Pie tins or other trays
- Plastic spoons
- Small recycled containers (clear jars or small plastic cups work best)
- Measuring cups

Directions:

This recipe is for <u>adults</u> to prepare ahead of time for collage or lacing activities. Fill several small containers with rubbing alcohol (1 per color). Add food coloring according to tone of color desired—pale or rich. Add uncooked pasta to the colored liquid, mix lightly and let set for 5 to 10 minutes (longer for richer color). Frequently mix and check for desired color. While waiting, line pie tins or trays with 3 to 4 paper towels (for each color). Once the pasta is desired color, spoon pasta into lined pie tins or trays to dry and drain. Frequently, separate pasta pieces as they are drying to prevent from sticking to one another and cracking. May need to change out paper towels if they are too wet, so pasta can dry evenly. Once pasta is completely dry, store in recycled containers.

CHAPTER 6

ACTIVITIES FOR EARLY LEARNING

Cookie Cutter Play Dough

Developmental Objective:
Sensory Motor – Touch, Smell, Taste
Language Development – introduce words; mix, blend, squeeze, knead, roll, smooth, oily, salty, bitter, shake, push, pour, stir, rough, smooth, squishy
Cognitive – Learn colors, counting, Learn concept of liquid and powder substances to solid matter, measurements

Age Focus: 2 years to 5 years-old

Materials:
· 1 large mixing bowl
· Vegetable Oil
· Measuring cups (glass) and spoons
· Salt
· 1 Spatula
· Water
· All Purpose flour
· Small, child size rolling pin
· Food coloring
· Cookie cutters, garlic press, plastic knife or popsicle sticks for cutting play dough, other safe kitchen gadgets
· 2 small/medium size storage containers
· Plastic/wooden spoon
· Plastic mat/cookie sheet

Instructions:
Pour ¼ cup of flour into a small bowl and set aside. Pour 2 cups of flour and 1 cup of salt in a large bowl and stir. Pour 2 tablespoons of vegetable oil into the mixture and stir again. Measure 2 cups of slightly warm water into a glass measuring cup. Squeeze 6 to 8 drops of food coloring into the glass measuring cup. Make sure the colored water is a deep rich

color (protect clothing from stain). Slowly pour ½ cup of the colored water into the mixing bowl and mix all ingredients with a spoon. Slowly pour another ½ cup of water into the bowl and mix again. If mixture is still too dry, slowly add more colored water until the ingredients starts to thicken. At the point when the mixture is not too gooey, squeeze and knead the dough. Add colored water or flour until you have the desired texture of play dough. Remove all mixing items and put out all the kitchen gadgets listed above. Place small rolling pins on the plastic mats or plastic cookie sheets to play with the play dough. Store in an airtight container and keep refrigerated.

Mixing Techniques:
Allow the child to help as much as possible. Allow for spills. Encourage child to smell, feel and taste ingredients as you are making the play dough.

Variations:
• Substitute flour with corn meal for different texture
• Add used coffee grounds to flour for different texture
• For scented play dough add lemon, cinnamon, peppermint, orange, vanilla, almond etc. to ingredients

Bakers Clay

Developmental Objective:
Sensory Motor – Touch, Smell, Taste
Language Development – introduce words; mix, blend, squeeze, knead, roll, smooth, oily, salty, bitter, shake, push, pour, stir, rough, smooth, slimy, gooey
Cognitive – Learn colors, counting, shapes; learn concept of liquid and powder substances to solid matter; Learn measurements - cups, teaspoon

Age Focus: 2 years to 5-years-old

Materials:
· 1 large mixing bowl
· 1 Spatula
· Measuring cups (glass)
· 1 Baking cookie sheet
· Salt
· 2 small/medium size plastic/wooden spoon
· All Purpose flour
· Various colors of tempera paints
· Water
· Small paint brushes
· Cookie cutters
· Aluminum foil
· Various food flavorings

Instructions:
Pour 4 cups of flour into a large mixing bowl. Add 1 cup of salt. Add 1 ½ cups of water. Mix ingredients with a spoon or spatula. Knead dough and form into various shapes or use cookie cutters to make shapes. Place shapes on a baker's cookie sheet lined with foil and bake at 350 degrees for about 1 hour. Remove from oven and allow to cool. Paint when cool.

Mixing Techniques:
Allow the child to help as much as possible. Allow for spills. Encourage child to smell, feel and taste ingredients as you are making the baker's clay (before painting).

Variations:
• Use this to make shapes/forms relative to holidays. To make hanging ornaments push one end of a paperclip into the dough before baking. Once the shape is baked cooled and painted you can put string, yarn or ribbon through the exposed loop of the paperclip. After painting shake some glitter on wet paint to add sparkle.
• To make necklaces, roll a very small ball of clay and use the rubber end of a pencil to make a hole in the middle of the ball. Bake, cool and paint. Now ready to lace with string or yarn to make a necklace or bracelet.

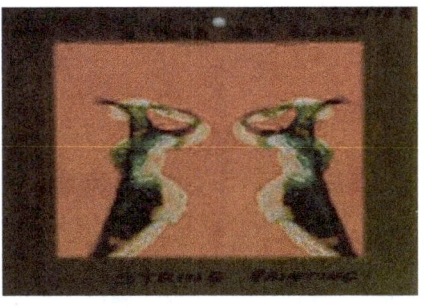

String Painting

Developmental Objective:

Sensory – Touch, visual

Physical – Fine motor, eye-hand coordination

Language – Introduce words, blend, push, press, pull, slowly, rub, turn, fold

Cognitive – Learn colors; primary and secondary, shapes, right, left, top, bottom, over, under

Age Focus: 2.5 years to 5 years-old

Materials:

○ Paints (Primary colors)

○ 8x11, white/colored paper (can cut into various shapes)

○ Small paint brushes

○ Different sizes of yarn (3 or less)

○ Clothes pins

○ Trays/recycled food cans for paint (empty meat trays; pie pans, etc.)

○ Absorbent material for trays (i.e., paper towel doubled, very thin spongy material, etc.)

○ Aprons

○ Newspaper

○ Tub of water to wash hands w/ paper towels

Instruction:
Prepare activity:
Cover table with newspaper or a tablecloth. Use 2-3 trays and line each one with absorbent material. Pour individual colored paint into its own tray on top of the material; just enough to lightly soak material completely with paint. Gather 2-3 strands of yarn and 2-3 clothespins and tie one end of each yarn to the bottom end of each clothespin with a knot. Place the untied end of each yarn into the paint of each tray. Make sure the clothespin is hanging outside of the tray/can, so that it stays dry of paint. Use a small paint brush, if necessary, to cover the yarn completely with paint. Put on aprons. Have a tub of water with paper towels nearby for hand washing. After the activity is completed, the clothespins with yarn can be cleaned, dried and stored for reuse.

Instruction to Child(ren):
Take one paper and fold it in half. Place the folded paper flat on the table and open it from right to left (like turning a page of a book). Choose a clothespin, one at a time, from each of the different colors of paint and place the yarns in any design on ONLY the right side of the paper with the clothespin placed anywhere OFF of the right side of the paper (top, side or bottom).

After you are done placing the painted yarn onto the paper, fold the left-side of the paper to the right side of the paper (like closing a book), over the yarns. Press and rub over the paper, with either hand, from the bottom to the top about 2 times. After, continue pressing with one opened-hand on the middle of the paper, feeling the paper and strings under the hand. Using the other hand, grab one clothespin at a time and slowly pull the yarn out of the folded paper. Place each colored yarn back into the matching color tray/can with the clothespin hanging outside the tray. After all yarns are removed from the folded paper, open it from right to left and see various blended colors.

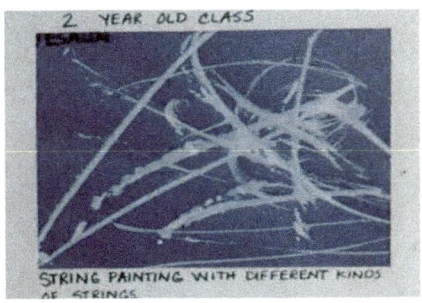

STRING PAINTING WITH DIFFERENT KINDS OF STRINGS

Variation:

Paint with strings of various thickness. Paint with or without strings tied to a clothespin. Paint over entire flat paper with strings, without folding.

Marble Painting

Developmental Objective:
Sensory Motor – Touch, visual
Physical Development - Large and fine motor, eye-hand coordination
Language Development – Introduce words; mix, blend, pour, slowly, roll, scoop, both, balance, lift, tilt, back and forth, side to side
Cognitive – Learn colors; primary and secondary, right, left, back and forth, up and down

Age Focus: 3 to 5 years-old

Materials:
○ Paints (Primary colors)
○ Light-colored paper (cut into circle shapes)
Marbles
○ Pie pans
○ Small cans/containers
○ Plastic spoons
○ Tape
○ Aprons
○ Newspaper
○ Tub of water to wash hands with paper towels

Instruction:
Prepare activity:
Cover table with newspaper or a tablecloth. Cut several paper circles that are the same diameter as the middle of the pie pans being used. Line the pie pan with 1 circle-shaped paper. Cut one piece of tape and roll it so it is sticky on both sides, then place it on the back of the circle and press in the center of the pie pan to keep the paper in place. Use 2-3 colors of paint and pour into individual small cans/containers and add 3 small marbles to each can/container. Place 1 plastic spoon inside each can/container. Have a tub of water with paper towels nearby for hand washing. Put on aprons.

Instruction to Child(ren):
Take a plastic spoon (one for each color of paint) and scoop up 1-2 marbles from each of the 2 to 3 different colors of paint. Pour the painted marbles onto the paper, inside the pie pan. Place the plastic spoon back into the matched color of the can/container. When done, using both hands, hold the left and right edge of the pie pan and slowly tilt the pie pan back and forth and up and down. Use your eyes and hands to keep the painted marbles inside the pie pan. Once the marbles have no more paint on them you can chose a color and scoop up one spoonful of paint. Drip the paint into the middle of the pie pan, put the spoon back into the can/container of paint and continue to roll the marbles back and forth; side to side (repeat with other colors if desired).

Wheel Painting

Developmental Objective:
Sensory Motor – Touch, visual, eye-hand coordination
Language Development – Introduce words; mix, blend, slowly, roll
Cognitive – Learn colors; primary and secondary, right, left, back and forth, up and down, lines, crisscross, across

Age Focus: 2.5 to 5 years-old

Materials:
- Paints (Primary colors)
- Light-colored paper (8x11 or a bit larger)
- Small toy cars/trucks
- Trays for paint
- Absorbent material for trays
- Aprons
- Newspaper
- Tub of water to wash hands w/ paper towels

Instruction:
Prepare activity:
Cover table with newspaper or a tablecloth. Use any type of light-colored paper. Line each tray with absorbent material. Pour 2-3 colored paints into individual trays, on top of the material; just enough to soak material completely with paint. Place 2 to 3 toy cars/trucks into each tray. Have a tub of water with paper towels nearby for hand washing. Put on aprons.

Instruction to Child(ren):
Take 1 car from a tray and roll the wheels of the car back and forth over the paint in the tray. Then place the car/truck with the painted wheels onto the paper and roll the toy car/truck back and forth or up and down to make different lines and lines that crisscross. Once the toy cars/trucks

have no more paint on the wheels, wet the car/truck wheels again in the same-colored paint they were in and repeat.

~

Sponge & Gadget Painting

Developmental Objective:
Sensory Motor – Touch, visual
Physical (Motor) Development – fine-motor, eye-hand coordination
Language Development – Introduce words; mix, blend, slowly, press, lift
Cognitive – Learn colors; primary and secondary, right, left, up and down, press, push

Age Focus: 2.5 to 5 years-old

Materials:
○ Paints (Primary colors)
○ Light-colored paper
○ various painting objects (small sponge pieces cut into various shapes, various sizes plastic lids, wood pieces, symbols, small cookie cutters, small spools, kitchen utensils etc.)
○ 3-4 Trays for paint
○ Absorbent material for trays (thin, yet spongy to prevent runny paint)
○ Aprons
○ Newspaper
○ Tub of water to wash hands w/ paper towels

Instruction:
Prepare activity:
Cover table with newspaper or a tablecloth. Use any type of white or light-colored paper. Line each tray with absorbent material. Pour individual colored paint into each tray covering top of the absorbent material just enough to soak material completely with paint. Place various painting objects into each tray. Have a tub of water with paper towels nearby for hand washing. Put on aprons.

Instruction to Child(ren):
Lift one object at a time from trays of paint and press the object into the paint and then lift the object and press it onto the paper. Lift the object put it back into the same-colored tray. Use various objects, from the other trays and repeat the process.

Eye Dropper Painting

Developmental Objective:
Sensory Motor – Touch, visual,
Physical Development - Fine motor, pinching, eye-hand coordination
Language Development – Introduce words; mix, squeeze, pinch, slowly, jar, container, release, liquid, change
Cognitive – Learn colors; primary and secondary, up, down, cause and effect, increase attention span

Age Focus: 3 to 5 years-old

Materials:
○ Water
○ Paper towels doubled
○ 2-3 Eye droppers
○ 2-3 Small glass jars or other type of container
○ Rubbing alcohol
○ Food coloring
○ Aprons
○ Tablecloth/ Newspaper
○ Tub of water to wash hands with paper towels

Instruction:
Prepare activity:
Cover table with newspaper or a tablecloth (strongly suggest newspaper if available). Use any shape of paper towel doubled. Add rubbing alcohol **or** water into a small glass jar (*baby food jars work great for this activity and can be saved to use again*) and then add drops of food coloring and mix (*supervise this activity if you use rubbing alcohol*). Place a different eye dropper into each jar. Have a tub of water with paper towels nearby for hand washing. Put on aprons.

Instruction to Child(ren):
Take one eye dropper at a time from the jar. With your fingers, pinch/squeeze up some of the colored liquid into the eye dropper tube. Place the eye dropper over the paper towel and release the colored liquid out SLOWLY, little bit at a time, over different areas of the paper towel. Repeat the process using different colors (the concept of pinching/squeezing and releasing slowly for young children takes practice; only encourage)

L.A.U.G.H. DAY CARE CENTER
2 YEAR OLD CLASS

VALENTINE HEART COLLAGE

Collage

Developmental Objective:
Sensory Motor – Touch, visual,
Physical (motor) development – Fine motor, eye-hand coordination
Language Development – Introduce words; cut, mix, squeeze, brush, container, stack, press, sticky, same
Cognitive – Experiment, creative development, judgment, insight, cause and effect, increase attention span, same, different

Age Focus: 3 to 5 years-old

Materials:
○ Glue
○ Cardboard, heavy paper, wood, boxes etc.
○ 2-3 small, recycled containers
○ Paint/food coloring
○ 2-3 Glue brushes
○ Large tray
○ Various recycled items, packaging, corks, bottle caps, shiny paper strips, ribbons, various colored string, yarn, small papers, egg carton rounds, other small objects
○ Aprons
○ Newspaper
○ Tub of water to wash hands with paper towels

Instruction:
Prepare activity:
Cover table with newspaper or a tablecloth. Half fill 2-3 small, recycled container with colored glue (See Basic Art Recipes section). Mix with glue brush. Place a glue brush into each container. Place a variety of objects onto the tray and place it in the middle of the table for easy access. Have a tub of water with paper towels nearby for hand washing. Put on aprons.

Instruction to Child(ren):
Use different colors of glue for the activity. When done using the glue brush, place it into the container that matches the same color. Choose several items from the tray and glue them to the cardboard, paper, large box or wood. Continue the same process until done.

Variations:
Collage with words and pictures from outdated magazines, old books, advertisement ads from newspaper, various grains etc.

Preparation:
• Ahead of time, cut out pictures and large print of words that pertain to a specific category for gluing. For example: animals - wild, domestic, ocean, birds, reptiles etc.; insects; dinosaurs; foods - fruits, vegetables, meats; flowers - gardens, trees; and vehicles - transportation, etc.
• Color some grains ahead of time: colored rice and various shapes of pasta (See Basic Art Recipes section)
• Have child glue them to the cardboard, paper, large box or wood.

Lacing & Sewing

Developmental Objective:
Sensory Motor – Touch, visual
Physical Development – Fine motor, eye-hand coordination, asymmetrical bilateral integration, bilateral coordination
Language Development – Introduce words; push through, pull out, edge, flip, next to, lace, front, back, near
Cognitive – Following directions, dimensional, increase attention span, shapes, symbols, next to, near

Age Focus: 3 to 5 years-old

Materials:
○ Any type of thick paper, cardboard, used greeting cards, light-weight plastic
○ Strawberry baskets or other food containers/objects with holes for lacing
○ Various colors and textures of heavy string, yarn, jute, ribbon, shoelaces etc.
○ Hole puncher
○ Scissors
○ Tape
Instruction:
Prepare activity:

Cut thick paper, cardboard etc., into various shapes (optional). Hole punch all around the edge of the paper, cardboard etc., with 3 finger spacing between holes. **Note:** 2 or 1 finger spacing can be made as a child grasps concept of lacing; graduating to the concept of loose sewing. Use scissors to cut long lengths of string, yarn, jute etc. (arm's length) Wrap tightly, one of the ends of string with tape (to mimic the end of a shoelace). Lace the other end of the string, yarn etc., through 1 of the holes and tie in a knot. This will keep the lacing material in place as the child laces around the paper, cardboard etc.

Note: If you are using thin paper, to prevent holes tearing from lacing: reinforce edges of paper with masking or packaging tape BEFORE punching holes around the edge of the paper.

Instruction to Child(ren):
With 1 hand, hold up the paper, cardboard (etc.) with holes in it. With the other hand, grab the end of the string with tape around it and push it through a hole. Slightly flip the paper with your hand, so you can see the other side of the paper. With the other hand pull the string until it stops. Flip the paper back to the front. With your fingers, push the end of the string through the hole next to the hole you just laced, slightly flip the paper and pull the string until it stops. Flip the paper back to the front and repeat with the next hole.

Advanced Variations:
Once a child learns the concept of lacing, add this to the activity: **Hand Sewing**

Materials:
○ Same sized squares of various loose knitted material (gauze, cotton, sweater, etc.)
○ Blunted yarn needles with long eye (plastic or metal)
○ Various colors and textures of string or yarn
○ Scissors

Instruction:

Prepare activity:

Using scissors, cut long lengths of string or yarn (arm's length). Cut evenly 2 squares of material (1 set per person). Push one end of the string/yarn through the eye of the needle and tie both ends of the string/yarn into a knot. Place squares of material into a tray and place in the middle of the table for easy access.

Instruction to Child(ren):

Chose 2 squares from the tray. Line up squares together so they are even. You can start sewing at any corner of the square. With one hand hold the 2 squares together NEAR (close to) the corner. Take your needle and push it through the corner of both squares. Slightly flip the squares with your hand, so you can see the other side of it. With the other hand pull the string or yarn until it stops. Flip the square back to the front. Push the needle through the material next to where you just sewed, slightly flip the square and pull the string until it stops. Flip the square back to the front and repeat. (Items made can be used for pockets, purses/satchels, potholders, coasters etc.)

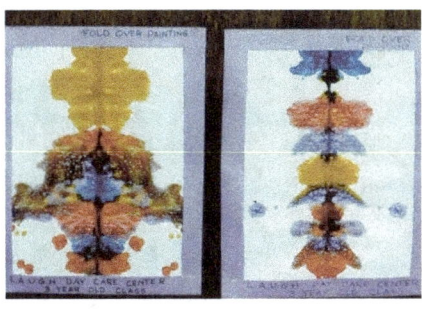

Fold Over Painting

Developmental Objective:
Sensory Motor – Touch, visual
Physical Development – Fine motor, eye-hand coordination
Language Development – Introduce words, blend, pour, push, rub, turn, fold, dab
Cognitive – Learn colors; primary and secondary, shapes, right, left, top, bottom, over, up, down, side-to-side

Age Focus: 3 years to 5 years-old

Materials:
○ Paints (Primary colors)
○ 8x11, white/colored paper (can cut into various shapes)
○ Various sizes of paint brushes
○ Recycled food cans for paint
○ Aprons
○ Newspaper
○ Tub of water to wash hands with paper towels

Instruction:
Prepare activity:
Cover table with newspaper or a tablecloth. Half-fill 3 to 4 recycled food cans with individual-colored paints. Place 1 – 2 different sized paint

brushes into each can. Put on aprons. Have a tub of water with paper towels nearby for hand washing.

Instruction to Child(ren):
Take one paper and fold it in half from left to right (like closing a book). Place the folded paper flat on the table and open it from right to left (like turning a page of a book). Take any paint brush from a can and dab some paint anywhere **ONLY on the right** side of the paper. Put the paint brush back into the can with the same-colored paint. Take a brush from a different can of paint and dab paint anywhere **ONLY on the right** side of the paper. Repeat this 4 times. After putting the paint brush into the same- colored can, fold the left side of the paper over to the right side of the paper (like closing a book). Press and rub over the paper, with either or both hands from the bottom to the top of the paper about 2 times. Press and rub over the paper with either or both hands from side-to-side about 2 times. Open the folded paper from right to left and see the various blended colors.

Stained Glass Melt

Developmental Objective:

Sensory – Touch, visual

Physical – Fine and gross motor, eye-hand coordination

Language – Introduce words, blend, push, press, slowly, rub, turn, spread, sprinkle, second

Cognitive – Learn colors; primary and secondary, shapes, right, left, top, bottom, over, attention span

Age Focus: 2.5 years to 5 years-old

Stained Glass Melt

Materials:

○ Primary colored crayons, pieces (preferably thick crayons; great to use with broken crayons)

○ 8 x 11 wax paper

○ Pie tins

○ Cheese grater

○ Variety of leaves, pressed flowers, flower petals

○ Trays (empty meat trays; pie pans, etc.)

○ Old Iron

○ Aprons

○ Newspaper/tablecloth

○ Tub of water to wash hands w/ paper towels

Instruction:
Prepare activity:
Cover table with newspaper or tablecloth. Cut 2 equal sized squares, rectangles or other shaped wax papers (2 per participant). Remove paper from selected crayons. Place crayons into tray and place in the middle of the table for easy access. Place pressed flowers, flower petals or leaves into another tray and place in the middle of the table. In a pie tin, place a cheese grater in the middle. Keep the iron unplugged until the end of the activity process for safety purposes. Put on aprons. Have a tub of water with paper towels nearby for hand washing. This activity requires constant supervision.

Instruction to Child(ren):
Select 3 to 4 crayons from the tray. Keep the cheese grater inside the pie tin. Using one color at a time, rub the crayon up and down on top of the cheese grater. The small, grated pieces will fall into the pie tin. Repeat until all the selected pieces have been grated. Set the cheese grater aside and leave the grated crayons inside the pie tin. Select 3-4 combination of leaves, pressed flowers or flower petals from the tray. Take 1 piece of wax paper and arrange the selected flowers, petals and leaves any way desired and leave in place. With finger tips gather the grated crayon pieces a little bit at a time. Sprinkle the pieces over the flowers, petals and leaves that are on the wax paper and leave in place. Take a second piece of wax paper and place it over the wax paper with flowers, petals, leaves and grated crayon pieces.

Adult Supervision Instruction:
Adult will sit next to the child and plug in the old iron to <u>warm</u>. Explain to the child that only an adult can use an iron and why. Have the child place one of their hands on top of the adult's hand that is holding the handle of the iron. Have the child sit on the other hand they are not using. Adult will slowly iron over both pieces of wax paper, melting the grated pieces of crayon and binding the 2 pieces of wax paper together

with the warmed iron. Have the child remove their hand from the adult's hand and place that hand under the table, while the adult removes the iron, from the table, unplugs it and keeps it away from close range of the child. After the wax paper cools in a few seconds, hold the paper up to a window or light and see the designs of melted colors with the flowers, petals and leaves that resemble stained glass.

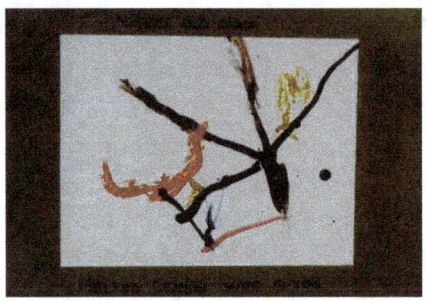

Melted Crayons

Materials:
- Various colored crayons (no less than half long crayons)
- Trays (empty meat trays; pie pans, etc.)
- Aluminum foil
- Any type of paper 8 x 11 or larger
- Masking tape
- Old hot plate/food warmer
- Aprons
- Newspaper/tablecloth
- Tub of water to wash hands with paper towels

Instruction:
Prepare activity:
Cover table with newspaper or tablecloth. Cut equal sized squared, rectangle or other shaped paper. Remove paper from selected crayons that are half-sized or longer (no shorter than half-sized). Place crayons into tray and place next to hot plate for easy access. Prepare hot plate: cover hot plate with foil. Place a paper on top of the foil and use masking tape on the corners of the paper to hold in place. Plug in hot plate/food warmer to the low to medium setting. Put on aprons. Have a

tub of water with paper towels nearby for hand washing. This activity requires constant supervision.

Instruction to Child(ren):
Select 1 crayon at a time from the tray. Using one color at a time, hold the TIP of the crayon with fingers and very SLOWLY, draw on the paper that is on top of the hot plate and watch the crayon melt. Repeat with different colored crayons.

Variation:
Instead of using plain paper also use aluminum foil, wax paper or light-gauged sandpaper.

Painting

Developmental Objective:
Sensory – Touch, visual
Physical – Fine motor, eye-hand coordination
Language – Introduce words, blend, up, down, side to side, dab, smooth
Cognitive – Learn colors; primary and secondary, right, left, top, bottom

Age Focus: 2 years to 5 years-old

Materials:
○ Paints – various colors
○ 20x23, easel paper (can cut into various shapes/designs)
○ Various types of paper
○ Large, small, wide/thin tipped paint brushes
○ Paint cups, recycled food cans other type of containers
○ Aprons
○ Newspaper
○ Easel (optional)
○ Tub of water and paper towels to wash hands

Instruction:
Prepare activity:

Set up an easel or cover table with newspaper or a tablecloth. Pour individual colored paint into cups or recycled cans. Place 2-3 different sized paint brushes into individual containers of paint. Put on aprons. Have a tub of water with paper towels nearby for hand washing.

Instruction to Child(ren):
Use one paint brush at a time. Paint on the paper. Put the paint brush back into the container with the same-colored paint.

Variation:
Paint with small rollers, old toothbrushes, Q-tips, straws—experiment with other objects. Use various textures of paper to paint—sandpaper, corrugated paper, cloth paper, cardboard, various shaped small boxes, etc.

4 YEAR OLD CLASS

FINGER PAINTING WITH CORNMEAL

Finger Painting

Developmental Objective:
Sensory – Touch, visual
Physical – Fine motor, eye-hand coordination
Language – Introduce words, blend, up, down, side to side, drizzle, smooth, slide, slippery
Cognitive – Learn colors; primary and secondary, right, left, top, bottom

Age Focus: 2 years to 5 years-old

Materials:
○ Paints – Primary colors
○ 8.5x14 glossy paper or glossy poster board
○ Small plastic teaspoons
○ Paint cups or small recycle cans
○ Aprons
○ Tablecloth
○ Shaving cream or Dawn dish soap
○ Optional--Sand, corn meal, breadcrumbs, used coffee grounds
○ Tub of water and paper towels to wash hands

Instruction:
Prepare activity:

Cover table with a tablecloth. Pour individual colored paint into paint cups or recycled cans. Place plastic spoons into individual containers of paint. If using optional items, put sand corn meal etc. into individual trays with a plastic spoon. Place paper on table. Place can of shaving cream or bottle of dish soap next to the paper. Put on aprons. Have a tub of water with paper towels nearby for hand washing.

Instruction to Child(ren):
Squirt plenty of shaving cream/dish soap onto various places of the paper. Scoop 1 teaspoon of paint and drizzle over shaving cream or dish soap. Repeat with remaining colors of paint. Place your fingers from both hands into the mixture on the paper and paint all around the paper with your fingers. Optional – add a different texture by sprinkling 1 teaspoon of sand, corn meal, coffee grounds etc. to the finger paint.

Variation:
• Homemade finger paints (See Basic Art Recipes – Chapter 5). The ingredients are the same EXCEPT, paint, dish soap, shaving cream are NOT required. Optional ingredients can still be used to add different textures.
• Finger paint ingredients that can be eaten. Use whip cream or pudding ONLY and add food coloring to make different colors. Licking finger can be fun after painting is done. Optional ingredients are not recommended UNLESS it is a food product that can be eaten safely.

Spin Art Painting

Developmental Objective:
Sensory Motor – Touch, visual
Physical Development- Large and fine motor, eye-hand coordination
Language Development – Introduce words; mix, blend, pour, slowly, scoop, spin, around
Cognitive – Learn colors; primary and secondary, right to left, left to right, cause and effect

Age Focus: 3 to 5 years-old

Materials:
○ Paints (Primary colors)
○ Light-colored paper (cut into circle shapes) or white paper plates
○ Old salad spinner
○ Small cans/containers
○ Plastic spoons
○ Aprons
○ Newspaper
○ Tub of water to wash hands w/ paper towels

Instruction:
Prepare activity:
Cover table with newspaper or a tablecloth. Cut several paper circles that are the same diameter as the middle of the salad spinner basket (if using paper plates, trim to size). Place circle paper or paper plate into the salad spinner basket. Use 2-3 primary colors of paint and pour into individual small cans/containers. Place 1 plastic spoon inside each can/container with paint. Have a tub of water with paper towels nearby for hand washing. Put on aprons.

Instruction to Child(ren):
Take a plastic spoon (one for each color of paint) and scoop up 1

spoonful of paint and pour it onto the paper inside the salad spinner. Place the plastic spoon back into the matched color of the can/container. When done pouring all the scoops of paints onto the paper inside the basket, cover with the spinner's lid. Hold the spinner with one hand and turn the handle of the spinner from left to right or right to left, to spin the inside basket with your other hand. Spin it as fast as you can. When done, stop spinning and wait for the spinner to stop. Remove the spinner lid and carefully remove the paper from the basket to see your artwork. Set aside and allow to dry.

Variation:
Add 2-3 small marbles into the spinner basket before putting the lid on to spin and see what happens!

~

GLOSSARY OF EARLY CHILD DEVELOPMENT TERMS

1. Abstract Idea - An idea that does not have a physical or concrete form.

2. Asymmetrical Bilateral Integration - Both sides of the body and brain are involved. The dominant hand and non-dominant hand assist each other toward a common goal as seen in activities such as cutting with scissors, coloring, writing or stringing beads.

3. Attention Span - This plays an important role for a young child's cognitive development for learning, processing information as well as developing listening and analytical skills. Attention span increases with less distraction, as a child grows and develops.

4. Bilateral Coordination - Having the control to use both sides of the body in an organized way and shows that the left and right sides of the brain are working together and communicating.

5. Cognitive Development – How children think, explore and interact with people and objects in their environment and learn from their surroundings. It is the development of knowledge, skills and problem-solving that help children to think about and understand their relationship to the world around them.

6. Cognitive Literacy - Cognitive skills are the foundation for learning. These cognitive skills include attention, visual and auditory processing, as well as executive functions that include a working memory, self-control and flexible thinking which are all necessary for academic performance and life success.

7. Compare/Contrast – Attention to what is the same and different between two objects. The concept of comparing is looking at what is similar, and contrasting is looking at what is different.

8. Critical Thinking - The ability to engage in reflective and independent thinking. It requires an ability to reason. It is about being an active learner rather than a passive recipient of information.

9. Crossing the Mid-line - An integral skill related to bilateral coordination. It refers to the ability to naturally cross over the mid-line of the body during motor tasks- moving one hand, foot, or eye into the space of the other hand, foot, or eye (i.e., sitting with legs crossed, reading left to right, etc.). By 3-4 years of age, a child should typically have mastered the skill of crossing mid-line. Also, a child's establishment of hand dominance is an indicator their brain is maturing.

10. Developmental Domains – Children grow and develop rapidly in their first five years across the five main areas of development that include: cognitive, physical (motor), language/communication, social and emotional.

11. Early Childhood – A term defined as a time from birth to eight years of age that is the most intensive period of brain development. This period is the most critical time for the growth and development of a child.

12. Executive Functioning Skills (EFS) – A term that includes a working memory, self-control and flexible thinking which are all necessary for academic performance and are not fully developed until adulthood. Working memory is the ability to keep information in mind and then use it in some way. Flexible thinking is the ability to think about something in more than one way. Self-control is the ability to ignore distractions and resist temptation.

EFS Development from 0-12 months of age:

Working Memory - Babies begin to recognize, recall and remember familiar faces. They are able to store that information and retrieve it when they see a face. Attachment is influenced by working memory.

Favorite toys and soothing items and positions are influenced by working memory.

Emotional Control - Infants do not have the ability to control their emotions. Attachment and responding to one adult but not another is influenced by the initial development of emotional control as infants feel safe and loved by members of their family.

Attention Control - Infants are able to make eye contact and follow objects with their eyes. Attention is greatly developed in the first year.

EFS Development from 12-24 months:

Flexibility is a skill that develops greatly during these months. The ability to inhibit impulses, sustain attention, control emotions, goal persistence, working memory and utilize flexible thinking, begin to develop by age 2 and increases with age. At this stage, much of this development occurs through play and interactions with adults.

Organization is a skill a toddler develops to understand patterns and sort items by form, function, and classification.

Problem-solving is a skill infants and toddlers develop through play in trying to figure out how things work and increases with age.

Task Initiation is the ability to start a task in a timely manner. A child at this stage initiates playing with toys.

EFS Development in Preschool-age:

Preschool-age children, typically ages 3 to 5, are able to do simple errands using working memory, sustain attention, and goal persistence. They can understand and recall instructions.

EFS Development in grades K-2:

In these years of schooling, children are able to follow 2-3 step errands such as cleaning a room independently, simple chores, and multiple step grooming and dressing tasks.

EFS Development in grades 3-5:

Children are able to complete multiple step tasks and maintain sustained attention. They are able to read and follow chapter books that require extended working memory and start on projects that require sustained attention to achieve their goal (goal persistence). Flexibility is further improved.

EFS Development in grades 6-8:

A child's working memory develops as they are able to complete more complex tasks. They are able to perform multiple step math and word problems toward the end of this age range. Critical thinking improves between the ages of 6 and 8. Students exhibit increasing impulse control at school and other places where rules are in place.

13. Eye-Hand Coordination - Children use their eyes to coordinate their movements, handling and control of objects. This is also included in the area of fine motor skill.

14. Inductive Reasoning - A logical process that involves using experiences or observations to identify patterns and make a general conclusion.

15. Language/ Communication Development – Different ways a child understands and communicates through sounds, spoken words, use of sign language or other means to communicate with others.

16. Learning Styles - Children have preferred ways of learning by means of Auditory - learn best by listening and being told about things; Visual - learn best when shown how to do things; Tactile - learn best by using hands-on approach; Kinesthetic - learn best through movement and action. Children can learn through all or any combination of these learning styles.

17. Parallel Play – A form of play in which a very young child plays independently in the presence of another child or other children.

18. Perceptual Development - An aspect of cognitive development that allows a child to start interpreting and understanding sensory input, as they engage with the world around them and learn more about what they touch, see, smell, hear, and taste. The process of perceptual development is very closely linked to motor development, as a young child's ability to crawl and later walk, allows opportunities for purposeful engagement with the surrounding world.

19. Physical (Motor) Development – The physical growth and strengthening of a child's bones, muscles and ability to move and touch their surroundings. It includes two categories, Fine and Gross Motor skills: Fine motor skills involve small movements in the hands, wrists, fingers, feet, toes, lips and tongue. Children need to control the small muscles in their hands and fingers to handle things like scissors, a spoon, a crayon or to pick up an object. These skills are important for learning to write. Gross motor skills involve development of muscles that enable babies to hold up their heads, sit and crawl, scoot and eventually walk, run, jump and skip.

20. Problem-Solving Skills - The foundation of a young child's learning. Problem-solving is a crucial aspect of critical thinking, as it involves the process of working through a variety of ideas to reach a solution. This skill contributes to a child's language and social development which are necessary to allow children the ability to interact with others and to share and vocalize their ideas to help find the right solution.

21. Reasoning Skills - Reasoning in children is an essential part of their cognitive development that includes thinking skills to problem-solve, discuss logically and to examine and analyze new information. A young child is not yet able to use analysis to problem-solve and therefore cannot use critical thinking to assess any solution. Young children learn by a process of trial and error, so the best way to ensure a child's healthy cognitive development is to involve them in activities that allow them to experiment and develop their mental creativity. This will help a child to develop critical thinking and a sense of reason so they can become more successful in school and their future life.

22. Schemes - Thought patterns that are considered the basic building blocks, or cognitive structures, of intelligent behavior and developed as a way of organizing knowledge.

23. Self-Confidence - An expression of self-esteem. A child's self-confidence develops over time with experience of successes as they master their skills and abilities, during their growing years.

24. Self-Esteem - The way we think and feel about ourselves. Children begin to develop self-esteem early in life. They are dependent on their parents and other influencing adults in their life for validation that they are lovable, smart, capable and worthy enough. When children feel good about themselves and confident of their abilities, they are likely to be successful in school. Parents who show their children lots of love and acceptance, in general, have children with high self-esteem.

25. Self-regulation - The ability to understand and manage your own behavior and reactions. Self-regulation helps children learn, behave well, get along with others and become independent and begins to develop rapidly in the toddler and preschooler years.

26. Sensory Motor Development - Sensory skills and motor skills systems go hand in hand; you cannot have one without the other. Both systems drive the brain. It is critical for these skills to improve and develop to aid in behavior and academic learning. Sensory skills involve using the senses of smell, touch, vision, hearing, balance (inner ear), taste and awareness of where your body is in space (surroundings). All of these senses work together for overall sensory functioning. Motor skills include coordination of both sides of the body (bilateral coordination), muscle strength and tone, gross and fine motor skills, balance and posture, visual tracking and coordination, rhythm and timing.

27. Sequencing - The process of putting events, ideas, and objects in a logical order. We understand events in our lives by understanding the order in which they occur: the beginning, the middle and the end. Sequencing is an important skill in pre-reading, comprehension, writing, math and science.

28. Social competence - Refers to the social, emotional, and cognitive skills and behaviors that children need for successful social adjustment and can vary with the age of the child and with the demands of particular situations.

29. Social and Emotional Development - A developmental period when children learn to understand who they are; learn to express emotion and what they are feeling; and form and maintain relationships with others.

30. Spatial Awareness - A child's awareness of their body in space and their relationship to the objects in the space. It includes a sense of distance learned through movement and exploration; it develops muscle strength, coordination, self-confidence, and thinking skills; and it is linguistic as children learn positional vocabulary (i.e., over, under, next to, etc.) and use it with their bodies. This is how children begin to develop an understanding of direction, distance, and location.

31. Symbolic Thought - Children master the ability to picture, remember, understand, and replicate objects in their minds that are not immediately in front of them. Children can create mental images of objects and store them in their minds for later use in activities, such as drawing or pretend play.

32. Symbolic Play - This happens when a child starts to use objects to represent (or symbolize) other objects.

33. Visual and Auditory Processing - The brain's processes of recognizing and interpreting information taken in through the senses of sight and sound; the eyes and ears.

REFERENCES

AbilityPath. (n.d.). Children's Learning Styles. AbilityPath. https://abilitypath.org/ap-resources/childrens-learning-styles/

Auditory Learner: Characteristics & Benefits., (2022, September 06). Afrebo https://afrebo.ngontinh24.com/article/auditory-learner-characteristics-benefits

Auditory Learner: Characteristics & Benefits. (2022, January). Bay Atlantic University. https://bau.edu/blog/auditory-learner/

Borst, H. (2022, February 1). Piaget's Stages of Cognitive Development. Mindpath. https://www.mindpath.com/resource/piagets-stages-of-cognitive-development

Bosley, D. (2016, July 29). Piaget's Theory of Cognitive Development. In Psychology Dictionary. Retrieved December 4, 2022, from https://psychologydictionary.org/piagets-theory-of-cognitive-development

Burns, J. (2016, April 8). Technology to Improve Social and Emotional Learning. Michigan State University College of Education, Green and Write. https://education.msu.edu/green-and-write/2016/technology-to-improve-social-and-emotional-learning

Bybee, R. & Sund, B. (1982). Piaget for Educators. Waveland Press.

Cristina. (2021). Musical Intelligence – Activities for Auditory Learners. What Does Mama Say? https://whatdoesmamasay.com/activities-for-auditory-leaners/

Challenges for the Visual Learner. (2008, February 17). Weebhoys Education Discussion. https://weebhoyseducationdiscussion.blogspot.com/2008/02/challenges-for-visual-learners.html

Cherry, K. (2019, November 27). Overview of VARK Learning Styles. Verywell Mind. https://www.verywellmind.com/vark-learning-styles-2795156

Cherry, K. 2021, April 01). The Concrete Operational Stage of Cognitive Development. Verywell Mind. https://www.verywellmind.com/concrete-operational-stage-of-cognitive-development-2795458

Cherry, K. (2022, February 16). Jean Piaget Biography (1896-1980). Verywell Mind. https://www.verywellmind.com/jean-piaget-biography-1896-1980-2795549

Courage, M. & Troseth, G. (2016). Infants, Toddlers and Learning from Screen Media. Encyclopedia on Early Childhood Development. https://www.child-encyclopedia.com/pdf/expert/technology-early-childhood-education/according-experts/infants-toddlers-and-learning-screen-media

Elkind, D. (2009). The Hurried Child. Da Capo Lifelong Books.

Exploring the Different Learning Styles of Young Children. (2021, October 20). Mind-Champs. https://www.mindchamps.org/blog/exploring-the-different-learning-styles-of-young-children

Fairchild, B. (2016, December 29). Right Vs. Left Brain Children. Peas and the Pod Chiropractic. https://peaandthepodchiropractic.com/right-vs-left-brain-children

Feldman, D. H. (2003). Cognitive Development in Childhood. In R. M. Lerner, M. A.

References

Easterbrooks, & J. Mistry (Eds.), *Handbook of Psychology: Developmental Psychology,* Vol. 6 (pp. 195–210). John Wiley & Sons, Inc. https://doi.org/10.1002/0471264385.wei0608

Feldman, D. H. (2004). Piaget's Stages: The Unfinished Symphony of Cognitive Development. *New Ideas in Psychology, 22*(3), 175-231. doi:10.1016/j.newideapsych.2004.11.005

Fleming, G. (2020, August 26). *Make the Most of Your Tactile Learning Style.* ThoughtCo. https://www.thoughtco.com/tactile-learning-style-1857111

Gongala, S. (2022, September 19). *4 Stages of Cognitive Development.* Mom Junction. https://www.momjunction.com/articles/stages-of-cognitive_development_00349351

Hilton, W. (2020). *What is Your Child's Learning Style?* Hip Home School Moms. https://hiphomeschoolmoms.com/what-is-my-childs-learning-style

Lally, M. & Valentine-French, S. (2019). *Introduction to Lifespan Development: A Psychological Perspective.* Martha Lally, Suzanne Valentine-French. https://open.umn.edu/open textbooks/textbooks/540

Left Brain vs. Right Brain Characteristics Chart: Which Type Are You? (2021, December 28). Kindling Zing. https://kindlingzing.com/left-brain-vs-right-brain-characteristics-chart-which-type-are-you/

Leisman, G., Moustafa, A. A., & Shafir, T. (2016). Thinking, Walking, Talking: Integratory Motor and Cognitive Brain Function. *Frontiers in public health,* 94. https://www.frontiersin.org/articles/10.3389/fpubh.2016.00094/full

Lipoff, S. (2011, April 26). *Learning Styles and Children.* Funderstanding. https://www.funderstanding.com/theory/child-development/learning-styles-and-children

Mann, D. (2007). *Understanding Your Child's Learning Style.* WebMD. https://webmd.com/parenting/features/childs-learning-style

McLeod, S. A. (2018, January 14). *Concrete operational stage.* Simply Psychology. https://www.simplypsychology.org/concrete-operational.html

McLeod, S. A. (2018, June 06). *Jean Piaget's Theory of Cognitive Development.* Simply Psychology. https://www.simplypsychology.org/piaget.html

McLeod, S. A. (2022, August 18). *Piaget's Stages of Cognitive Development.* Simply Psychology. https://www.simplypsychology.org//piaget.html#:

Moloney, A. (2022). *Technology Impact On Child Growth & Development.* The Tot. https://www.thetot.com/baby/the-impact-of-technology-on-behavior

Perlson, L. (2022). *Understanding Your Child's Learning Style.* Dr. Lisa Parenting. https://drlisaparenting.com/wp-content/uploads/2022/03/Learning-Styles.pdf

Perry, D. B., & Kneas, K. M. (2012, April 16). Using Technology in the Early Childhood Classroom. https://englishangonline.blogspot/2012/04/by-kimberly-moore-kneas-ph.html

Plowman, L., & McPake, J. (2013). Seven myths about young children and technology. *Childhood Education, 89*(1), 27-33. https://doi.org/10.1080/00094056.2013.757490

Putri, D. (2022, February 28). *Know Your Child's Learning Style: Auditory, Visual or Kinesthetic?* School Zones. https://school-zones.com/your-childs-learning-style

Pyle, A. (2018). *Play-Based Learning: The Joy of Learning Through Play.* Centre of Excellence for Early Childhood Development. https://www.tdsb.on.ca/Portals/0/EarlyYears/docs/Info%20play-based-learning-info.pdf

Raptopoulou, A. (2020). Preschool Teachers' Perspectives and Use of Digital Game-Based Learning. https://www.cier.edu.gr/wp-content/uploads/Raptopoulou.pdf

Reynolds, A. (2018, December). *The Physical Impact of Technology on Children.* Hello Motherhood. https://www.hellomotherhood.com/the-physical-impact-of-technology-on-children-9664109.html

Roell, K. (2019, June 23). *Understanding Visual, Auditory, and Kinesthetic Learning Styles.* ThoughtCo. https://www.thoughtco.com/three-different-learning-styles-3212040

Roell, K. (2020, August 27). *The Kinesthetic Learning Style: Traits and Study Strategies.* ThoughtCo. https://www.thoughtco.com/the-kinesthetic-learning-style-3212046

Sarkun, M. (n.d.). *Jean Piaget's Theory of Cognitive Development.* Technopython. https://technopython.com/jean-piagets-theory-of-cognitive-development

Sing, M. (2022, June 4). *Characteristics of Visual Learners.* NumberDyslexia. https://numberdyslexia.com/characteristics-of-visual-learners

Small, G. W., Lee, J., Kaufman, A., Jalil, J., Siddarth, P., Gaddipati, H., Moody, T.D.., & Bookheimer, S.Y. (2022). Brain health consequences of digital technology use. *Dialogues in clinical neuroscience.* 179-187. https://doi.org/10.31887/DCNS.2020.22.2/gsmall

Smith, J & Browne, D.T. (2019, July 17). *Is Your Child Addicted to Screens? Here's What You Can Do About It.* The Conversation. https://theconversation.com/is-your-child-addicted-to-screens-heres-what-you-can-do-about-it-118316

Spreeuwenberg, R. (2022, February 18) *Why Parent Involvement is So Important in Early Childhood Education.* HiMama, Early Childhood Education Blog . https://www.himama.com/blog/why-parent-involvement-is-so-important-in-preschool/

Thompson, C. & Rudolph, L. (1996). *Counseling Children.* Brooks Cole.

Van Ness, V. (2022, March 3). *The Positive and Negative Effects of Technology on Kids.* We Have Kids. https://wehavekids.com/parenting/The-Positive-and-Negative-Effects-of-Technology-on-Kids

Vinney, C. (2022, February 11). *Can Children Understand the Difference Between Fantasy and Reality?* Verywell Mind. https://www.verywellmind.com/can-children-understand-the-difference-between-fantasy-and-reality-5217713

Weekly, S. (1979). *The Theories of Jean Piaget – What They Mean for Special Education.* [Master's Thesis, University of Wisconsin – La Crosse] University of Wisconsin – La Crosse Seminar Papers. https://minds.wisconsin.edu/handle/1793/55273

Werling, K. (2020). The Effects of Technology in Early Childhood. [Master's thesis, Northwestern College]. Northwestern College Research Commons. https://core.ac.uk/download/pdf/346167667.pdf

Wilson, K. (2022, May 24). *3 Learning Styles In Children.* AdSume. https://adsume.com/3-learning-styles-in-children